From the Slums to Royal Priesthood

Reverend Father Christopher Geh Kum

Ukiyoto Publishing

All global publishing rights are held by

Ukiyoto Publishing

Published in 2024

Content Copyright © Reverend Father Christopher Geh Kum

ISBN 9789367950159

All rights reserved.
No part of this publication may be reproduced, transmitted, or stored in a retrieval system, in any form by any means, electronic, mechanical, photocopying, recording or otherwise, without the prior permission of the publisher.

The moral rights of the author have been asserted.

This book is sold subject to the condition that it shall not by way of trade or otherwise, be lent, resold, hired out or otherwise circulated, without the publisher's prior consent, in any form of binding or cover other than that in which it is published.

www.ukiyoto.com

I dedicate this book to Almighty God for granting me the wisdom within these pages. I also dedicate it to all young people around the world, especially those in the Archdiocese of Douala who feel discouraged and have lost hope.

Finally, to my late father, John Kum, and all the departed members of my family.

FOREWORD

As the Archbishop of Douala, I have worked with many servants of the Lord, and Christopher is among those with whom I work directly. Our relationship has been very cordial for as long as I can remember. I have watched him grow in his interactions with people of all ages and backgrounds—old and young, men and women—and, most importantly, in his relationship with Jesus Christ, reaching a place where his heart deeply yearns for knowledge of the Lord's beauty. I have also observed how tenderly he cares for those under his guidance, many of whom have become well-established, young, and God-fearing individuals. Therefore, I sincerely appreciate his contributions to the Lord's vineyard and gladly accepted the invitation to write the foreword for his book.

"From the Slums to Royal Priesthood!" is an autobiography that reflects over 20 years of experience, long before the Lord called the author to the priesthood. It is a book with much to offer, as many people may find parallels to their own lives in Christopher's story. This book will significantly boost the morale of those who have faced similar trials and uplift the spirits of those who may be close to giving up on life, regardless of their circumstances. We live in a world where many judge others without understanding their backgrounds or struggles. Some may wish to trade places, forgetting that we are all unique, with different destinies.

"From the Slums to Royal Priesthood!" emphasises that behind every success story lies hard work, perseverance, authenticity, and a God-fearing spirit. Despite challenges, I find it meaningful that the Douala Archdiocese accepted Christopher for priestly formation. Having worked closely with him for many years, I can attest that his journey was indeed God-ordained. When God calls you, He protects and guides you to the right path, regardless of the circumstances. Christopher's tireless dedication to serving the Lord underscores the importance of this thoughtful and inspiring autobiography. I give him my fatherly blessings.

- Archbishop Samuel Kleda

Acknowledgements

I acknowledge the grace of God for creating me and enabling me to author this book through the maternal intercession of the Blessed Virgin Mary. Many thanks to my parents for my birth and rightful upbringing, and to my siblings for their unconditional love.

Special thanks go to Esi Okafor and all my colleagues at the School of Life. I also acknowledge the Legionaries for deepening my knowledge of God through the Blessed Virgin Mary after my conversion.

My sincere gratitude extends to Mr. & Mrs Ndefru Linus, Mr. & Mrs. Fanso, Mr. & Mrs. Galega, the Foudas, Ngus, Yaris, Ndums, and Litumbes for being God's instruments in guiding me toward my destiny.

Special thanks go to Mr. Elias Poungong and his family for being God-sent and a true brother, to Jeanette Monkam, and to Mr. & Mrs. Lebomo for their support in all my endeavours.

To the pilgrims, the chapel community, and all my adopted children, thank you for being the source of my happiness. I am grateful to the Ntams, Tamias, Tchangouns, Dayas, and Tinens for supporting me on my faith journey.

Thank you to all my special friends and well-wishers who have contributed in various ways to my life. May God reward you all with eternal happiness.

Contents

Chapter I - My Origin And Early Life	1
Chapter II - Life After My Grandfather's Death	10
Chapter III - Our Departure To Bamenda	16
Chapter IV - The Return Of Mr. Esi Okafor	27
Chapter V - My Spiritual Engagement	34
Chapter VI - I Am Made Manager Of A New Branch	41
Chapter VII - My Journey to the Village	46
Chapter VIII - My Return To Bamenda	51
Chapter IX - The Way Forward	56
Chapter X - Life After Esi Okafor	60
Chapter XI - Life In Yaoundé	68
Chapter XII - My New Life	73
Chapter XIII - My Turning Point	81
Chapter XIV - My Final Yes To God's Call	90
Glossary: Pidgin English And French Words and Phrases	100
About the Author	*102*

Chapter I - My Origin and Early Life

When God, in the presence of Angels and Saints, decided to send me into this world through my earthly parents, I had no say. He formed and placed me in my mother's womb, and while there, He looked after me (Ps 139:13, 15). As my Creator, He has known how long I would live and all I would experience, long before I was born (Ps 139:16). He knows everything about me, including my name. He is a mystery beyond human reason (Ps 139:1-6, Is 43:1, Sir 18:4). My God is such a great God; nothing compares to His greatness, and I am absolutely nothing without Him.

I learned from my parents, doctors, and those who lived before me that I was born on January 1, 1965, at the Aghem-Wum General Hospital. My parents, John Kum Kawzu of blessed memory and Ndum Paulina are both natives of the Esu Fondom of the North West Region of Cameroon. Thirty years after my birth, I was told of the unusual circumstances that surrounded it. My parents shared that my mother laboured for four days, and even when I arrived, it was feet first, with the placenta having to be torn to release me, unlike most children who come headfirst. My mother added that I had strange toes on the day I was born.

The mystery of life is that we are born empty, or unconscious, as the Empiricist philosopher suggests, and learn through life's experiences as we grow older.

I am the third of ten siblings from my mother; eight boys and two girls. In those days, marriages were often arranged between families. My mother's marriage to my father resulted from such an arrangement, as she was betrothed to him at a very young age to strengthen the friendship between their parents. She left her family home at thirteen to live with my father. Before this, my father had inherited his uncle's wife, who had given him two daughters. Sadly, she passed away a few years after my mother joined the household as my father's wife.

When my mother came to live with them, she was treated almost like a daughter by my father's uncle's wife, who was already a fully grown woman while my mother was only thirteen. After my mother, my father inherited four of his late brother's wives. According to the customs of our people at that time, this arrangement meant that he was "looking after" these women and many children joined the family as a result.

It was also common for the Fon to choose a wife from among the young women of the community, setting her aside as his wife with or without her consent. Sometimes, these women were even brought to him in the palace, and the girl's family could not object. The manner in which this was done could fill an entire book. Despite all this, my mother, the youngest of these women, remained the only authentic wife to my father. She was the only woman for whom he paid a bride price, solidifying her status as his official wife.

By nature, my parents were selfless, calm, understanding, and generous, especially my father. Unlike my mother, he was quieter and soft-spoken, and his wisdom won my admiration. He had a gift for comforting others, easily talking anyone out of their worries. He dreaded eating alone and would only eat when one of his children was nearby to share the meal. This fostered a strong sense of family love in us. He often sacrificed his own needs to ensure we had medical care and food. His family was his life's purpose. Although uneducated, he managed his family with remarkable tact, wisdom, and love. He taught us that love for the person next to us is the greatest gift to humanity and that love conquers all. Each of his children has inherited love, respect, or both from our father.

I am from a royal family of the Esu Fondom. The last Fon, His Royal Majesty Fon Kum-a-Chuo Albert Chi Kawzu II, was my brother and my mother's first son. When I was still very young, there was much talk about the next king of the village coming from among my father's children, though no one knew who it would be. My father taught us much about the responsibilities of a good leader, emphasizing that a good leader must be selfless,

Young Christopher Geh Kum

kind, and lead by example. He also impressed upon us that a good leader must be willing to serve and put the interests of others above their own. In other words, we learned that a leader is the first servant of his people.

My father often recounted the mysterious lives of our ancestors, who led with wisdom and strength. These stories about leadership inspired us to question whether we could truly fulfil the role of a good leader when the time came. This thought made us—especially me—quite fearful, as I dreaded the idea of becoming the leader of my people one day. Today, I praise God for choosing me for a greater assignment.

I was born into a typical Presbyterian family. My parents were practising Presbyterian Christians who held strongly to their faith, evident in the way we were baptized. My parents ensured all their children were baptized on or before the age of one. According to church records, I was baptized in the Presbyterian Church Naikom Over-side, Wum, on December 11, 1965 (card number 1568) by Reverend Pastor T.N. Chiangong.

My godparents were Clement and Cecilia Fru, charged with the responsibility of guiding and directing me in my Christian journey. Unfortunately for me, they did not do much in that regard. However, this did not bother me much because my parents were always there to shepherd us along the right path.

In our culture, the burden of raising children largely falls on the mothers. The father provides moral, spiritual, and limited financial support. My father inherited his brother's children when he took their mothers as concubines, leading to a household of more than forty-five children. Raising these children was not easy, but the social structure and my father's strong management skills kept our family united and instilled in us a spirit of love and respect.

My father's wives were each responsible for encouraging their children to work hard in school and at home, and for teaching them basic ethics, customs, and traditions. A child's attitude often depends on their mother's teachings. My mother, though she mostly had boys, taught us to do everything a girl could do. She showed us how to cook, plough the fields, harvest, fetch wood, and assist her with her kerosene and tobacco businesses. These small-scale ventures provided just enough to pay her church contributions, contribute to her "njangis," and purchase basic necessities like Maggi, palm oil, and salt.

In 1973, at the age of eight, arrangements had been made for me to begin school. However, when my stepmother gave birth, there was no one to look after my stepsister, Emilia Ndum, so I was asked to babysit her. Although it was difficult for me to accept, I respected my parents' decision. A year later, in September 1974, I began my formal education at Presbyterian Primary School in Wum at the age of nine.

Despite my late start, I was not the oldest pupil in my class—some of my classmates were between fifteen and eighteen years old. This was a relief for me during my first days at school. My early years in school were challenging. I could hardly boast of a proper school uniform, bag, or even textbooks. My worst experience was in primary five when my parents became so financially strained that we could not afford even basic necessities like Maggi (seasoning cubes). My father's carpentry business was not bringing in enough for the family.

I had no dresses or textbooks, and the only decent clothing I had was my school uniform, which had worn down to barely 30 per cent of its original condition when my parents first bought it.

I took on the responsibility for my education. I began selling raffia bamboo used for cooking. After school each day, especially during the planting season, my brothers and I would go home, change clothes, and join my mother at her farm, sometimes two to three kilometres from home. Planting season was the hardest time of the year, marked by severe food shortages that we nicknamed "twenty hungry." Mother would take our lunch to the farm as a way to motivate us to come along after school. Sometimes, lunch consisted of squeezed corn fufu with raffia wine or squeezed corn fufu with palm kernels. Going to the farm gave me the chance to collect raffia bamboo, which I later sold to make ends meet. Through this, I managed to pay my school fees, buy textbooks, and cover other school needs.

My parents were disciplinarians who always wanted the best for us. Correction was a way of life in our family. When I was in primary five, I took 25 FCFA from my mother's tobacco money without her knowledge or permission. She eventually found out, and it was the worst experience of my life, as my parents were deeply disappointed in me. They saw it as a curse to have a child who stole. I felt ashamed and received some strokes of the cane. That night, I didn't sleep in the house out of fear of more beatings and embarrassment. When I didn't return, my parents grew worried and searched for me everywhere. When they finally found me the next day, I saw great relief on their faces, replacing their worry and stress. I sensed they were beginning to consider other ways of disciplining us besides flogging. I disliked flogging as punishment, even when I was wrong. The incident remains fresh in my mind as if it happened yesterday. It taught me a lesson, and I resolved to avoid any actions that would bring disgrace to me and my family and to focus more on my studies. However, concentrating on my studies was still challenging in primary five due to my age and the influence of friends.

My school was surrounded by farms with fruits like mangoes, guavas, bananas, and oranges. Often, during lunch breaks and after school, my friends would persuade me to join them on these farms to pick fruit. I went along mainly to avoid being called a coward or weakling. I recall one time when the farm owners chased us with a machete and spear. Some classmates who recognized us reported directly to our parents, and each time they did, we faced severe punishments. These punishments only fueled feelings of revenge in my friends and me.

One time after school, my brothers, friends, and I went to a farmland to fetch firewood. Fortunately (or unfortunately for the farm owner), we met him there, and he stopped us from collecting wood. Already frustrated, we tied him to a tree and went about gathering firewood. When we finished, we untied him. He was furious but couldn't do anything, as we outnumbered him. Later, he reported us to my parents and threatened to take us to the police and the village chief. My parents pleaded with him not to go that far, promising to discipline us and offering some money as compensation. Believe me, we received the beating of our lives, just as my father had promised.

On other occasions, we visited sugarcane farms, tied ropes to the stalks, stood at a distance, and pulled the sugarcanes toward us. Whenever we did this while the farm owner was around, he would run, shocked to see the sugarcane moving as if by itself. They were often so frightened, thinking it was a ghost. These were always comic moments for us.

Later, in the second half of 1979, my paternal grandfather, Kawzu, fell ill and came to live with us. He was nearly a hundred years old but still looked remarkably young and strong for his age. In those days in the village, most kitchens had beds, so he decided to stay in my mother's kitchen and use the bamboo bed that was there. The doctors said he needed to stay warm, so I was asked to sleep with him and tend the fire in the kitchen whenever it went out.

During those years, the nights and mornings were so cold that one could barely feel their fingers and toes; fire was the only way to stay warm. I became a dedicated attendant to my grandfather, weakened by illness. Most nights, he would tell me stories about our family's history, our people, and the succession to the royal throne. He shared his experiences and the challenges he faced to become a successful leader. Having served in the Second World War, he recounted the awe-inspiring might of the Germans and his wartime experiences. I was captivated by his storytelling, and impressed by the clarity and coherence of his narratives. Since he slept little at night, he knew he could hold my attention best during those hours, as I slept beside him. Occasionally, I'd drift off as he spoke, but his stories would continue in my dreams. On nights when he shared particularly enthralling tales, I stayed awake until he finished, though fatigue would inevitably be my companion the next morning.

Focusing at school the next day wasn't always easy. Still, I loved my grandfather's stories—they taught me courage, the importance of listening more and speaking less, and, most importantly, the value of choosing my companions wisely. Many of his tales inspired me to become a hero, a defender of the downtrodden, and a champion of justice and equity. He often reminded me that those who fight for justice live with constant risk. My grandfather emphasized that a person should never be judged by appearances alone; he encouraged me to observe people's character carefully before forming conclusions or reacting. He likened the character to pregnancy—no matter how long it's hidden, a person's true nature will eventually show.

Grandpa, like my parents, was a disciplinarian. I later understood where my father got his disciplinary nature from. Being the closest person and companion to Grandpa was not always a bed of roses. We had our ugly moments. Each time I came home late, he would thrash me. He had a pinching broom with which he administered his punishment. Believe me, you would not want him to use that on you. I remember one time I came home late from playing football. Each time I played, I didn't notice time passing. When the game ended, the reality of time suddenly dawned on me. That unfortunate day, he was very furious because he needed my help earlier. As soon as I stepped into the kitchen, he grabbed me and, with his pinching broom, gave me the thrashing I deserved.

I managed to pull myself free from his grip and dashed out of the kitchen. Anger surged within me, and before I knew it, the words "stupid idiot" escaped my mouth. As soon as I said it, fear took hold—I knew the consequences. The entire family turned on me, taking turns to punish me and reminding me of my grandfather's greatness and importance. They made it clear that insulting him was an abomination. Guilt and fear settled in, and I felt deeply remorseful for my actions. Later, I asked for his forgiveness, which he graciously granted. In African tradition, parents and grandparents are revered, and respect for them is paramount.

In 1980, my grandfather's health further deteriorated. He lost most of his energy and cheerful attitude and became quieter, observing more. One night, he took me closer to himself and spoke to me faintly. I could barely hear him. I was frightened.

"Son," he began, "you are a brave boy. The world has many rotten bridges, deserts, and mountains that stand before you, but you will triumph over them all. I want you to be very careful with two things: money and women. These two things delay the prosperity of great men and destroy their destiny" (Prov. 7:21-26). He added, "My shadow will always be with you to keep you safe and see you through."

He spat on my head and palms and asked me to go back to sleep. It was customary at that time that when an elderly person blessed you under such circumstances, the next minute he or she would pass on. After receiving Grandpa's blessings, fear took over my whole body.

"Grandpa will surely die now," I thought. I did not sleep that night. I stayed up, ready to inform my parents as soon as something happened. But he was not going to die that night. He slept on while I worried, and I felt a bit relieved when I heard him snoring in the early hours of the morning. I told no one about the incident between Grandpa and me. I only recounted this story long after he had passed on. When my father heard the story, he just smiled. I felt as though he were telling himself, "If only you knew how lucky you are, my son." Later that year, Grandpa passed on, and it was one of the most difficult moments for the family. Even though he was already old, he was one of the greatest sources of inspiration to us. I had become too close to him, and many people, especially family members, worried about how I would survive without him.

When Grandpa died, his remains were transported from Wum to Esu. The funeral preparations were intense and carried out with great care and diligence. He was a respected figure in the village, not only as a prince but also as the son of one of our most revered kings, Kum Achuo I. His funeral was a grand affair, rich with colour, pomp, and pageantry. All the traditional rites befitting a king were performed on his burial day. Many notable figures and traditional rulers from neighbouring villages attended to pay their respects. Throughout the ceremony, his body was respectfully attended by specially chosen elders and dignitaries. Witnessing the grandeur of his funeral, one might wish to be part of the royal family to receive such honours when passing from this world to the next. Like Abraham, he was laid to rest with his ancestors.

Chapter II - Life After My Grandfather's Death

My grandfather's death left a threatening vacuum in my life. I became quieter and spent most of my time alone. My parents and family members observed this and feared the worst for me. To keep an eye on me, I took turns spending the night with my parents on different days of the week to prevent me from doing myself harm. It did not help much because I kept thinking of my grandfather, especially at night, and of all we shared during the moments he spent with us. As children, we forget and heal faster from our worries than adults do. My emotional breakdown and mourning did not last long, as other concerns took over my thoughts. My school program became increasingly demanding, coupled with a few distractions here and there from my classmates, playmates, and friends. Primary Five was particularly challenging as we were introduced to the First School Leaving Certificate (FSLC) syllabus.

I worried about school, how to raise my fees, and how to obtain didactic materials for my education. My parents did not have it easy. Family responsibilities kept piling on them as the days and years went by. Many younger siblings kept adding to the family, making matters more complicated. The family situation and living conditions grieved me. I needed to work hard in school and at home to help relieve their burden once I completed my education. Inspired by my grandfather's stories, I wanted to leave an indelible footprint for posterity, just like the brave men and women he constantly told me about—a good and inspiring story about me. Being God's miracle was my greatest ambition. I knew the journey toward greatness was not simple, and Primary Six and Seven had taught me that. The workload increased, or even doubled, along with the fact that my female classmates had started distracting me, significantly affecting my class performance.

A few weeks into my final year of Common Entrance Examinations for secondary school, my father summoned me to his quarters very early one Sunday morning. Each time one received such a summons, it indicated that something important was about to be announced. He always did this between 4:00 a.m. and 5:00 a.m. I asked myself many questions about the summons.

"My son," he began, "I hope you are working hard towards your Common Entrance Examinations. I pray that you will be among those who succeed in List 'A' so that it will be easy and smooth for you to gain admission to a Government Secondary School. Without this, it will be almost impossible for us to raise enough money to send you to a private secondary school, given our present family situation. And you know that there is no one you and I can rely on for any financial or material support."

This pronouncement sent chills through my whole body. I felt like sitting, standing, and crying at the same time. It left me shivering with a million unanswered questions.

"What if I don't pass in List 'A'? What will happen to my future? What will be my next option? Will I one day be a successful man? What will my future look like without secondary education?" These questions kept running through my mind as I slowly and sadly walked back to my mother's kitchen, where I slept. I went to bed, but in the following hours before dusk, I could not sleep. I was so confused and drained. My attitude in school changed in the few days that followed. I became more reserved and contemplative. It took some days and even weeks for me to come to terms with the reality my father was trying to paint for me and to accept the facts as he bluntly presented them.

The examinations came, and I took them. The results were released, and my name appeared on the "B" list. My fears resurfaced, and my father's fears were also confirmed. It was 1981. Darkness filled my life, and I immediately concluded that my dreams would never be achieved or realized. I blamed my father for telling me my fate earlier; it put fear instead of courage in me. I could not manage my fears. I kept wondering if my grandfather's prediction of me becoming a great person would come to fruition. I ignored the part that said I would not find it easy but would eventually succeed.

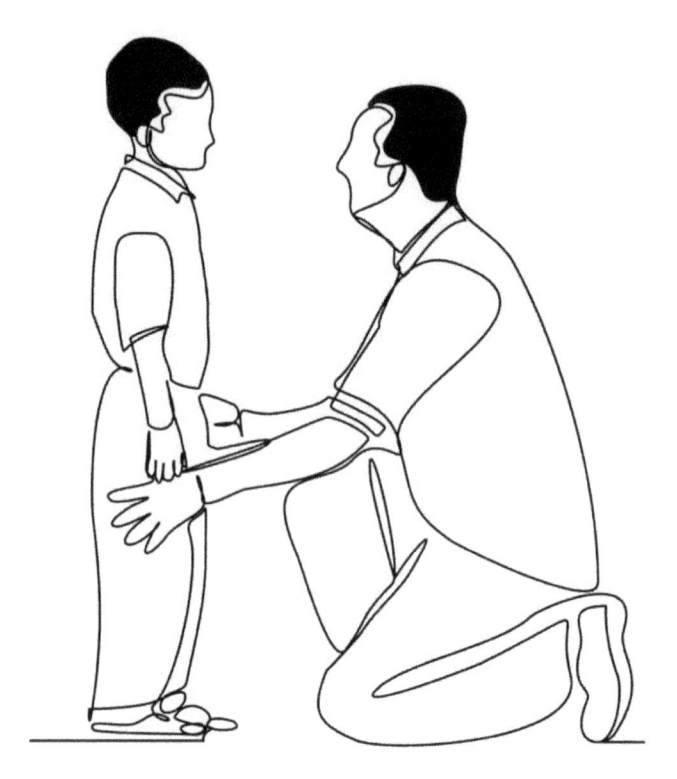

"Son, you cannot continue schooling due to our family's degrading financial situation."

The night after the results were released, I felt as if my grandfather were lying beside me, encouraging me to hold steadfast to my dreams, brave the odds, and stay focused on believing in myself. I felt rejuvenated and alive the next day. The words of Norman Vincent Peale best describe what I felt that night when he said, "Apparently, you never realize that some of those who failed to get high grades in school have been the greatest successes outside of school. Just because somebody gets an A in college doesn't make him the greatest man in the United States. It may stop after his diploma, and you start having your real A's in life."

He further advised that another way to overcome defeat, inferiority complex, or doubt is to turn to God in faith through prayer. I discovered solace and strength in the scriptures: "When your time of pain is over, I will bring about the future you hope for. I alone know the plans I have for you, plans to bring you prosperity and not harm…" (Jeremiah 29:10-14). These words performed miracles in my life beyond human imagination.

The school year 1981/1982 began, and I was not among those who went to college in the family. It did not bother me as much as it should have. What preoccupied me was where I would be and what I would do for a living. Before I knew it, my father finally broke the news about how I would occupy myself and his plans for my future.

"Son," he began in his usual calmness, "As I told you earlier, it is now clear that you cannot continue schooling due to our family's degrading financial situation. God in heaven makes life possible for every creature, even those in the desert. I have been troubled about what to do for you. As God would have it, I have finally found something wonderful for you. If you consider what I am about to tell you, I promise you, even your friends going to school will never attain your level of success."

He paused and thought for a while. My anxiety had grown, and I was eager to hear the good news that was about to drop from his lips. Then he spoke: "Son, I want you to work as a shepherd boy for a Fulani herdsman. The reward for your services each year will be a cow."

These words pierced my heart; I felt valueless and hurt. "How could my father do this to me?" I thought. I was so disappointed with myself and my life! I was dumbfounded for a while. The next thing I could remember after the announcement was my brothers and sisters hovering over me. Then I heard one of them faintly asking the others if I had gone into a fit. The shock of this pronouncement had left me confused. I don't know how I got to my mother's kitchen, where my brothers and sisters were eager to know what my father had told me. Recounting what my father had just told me to my mother, brothers, and sisters was difficult. I did so with a heavy heart, tear-filled eyes, and much sobbing. My mother did not make things easy for me, either. She wept throughout as I recounted what my father had just told me. She said, "Na so my own things di always bi," and she took a firm decision: *"Over my dead body, my pikin no fit be nganankoh. Yi get plenty pikin ndem, make yi send ndem for go doam."*

Seeing my mother upset made me even more worried. I felt my world crumbling around me. It was the first and last time I had seen my mother object to my father's plans. My uncles and aunts also objected to my father's decisions. Since my father was an understanding person, he never mentioned it again, and the matter died a natural death. My mother kept encouraging me to concentrate on my wood-selling venture so that I could save enough money to permit me to go to school the following academic year. I preferred her opinion to be a shepherd boy who would spend most of his time in the mountains and valleys grazing cattle. Being a shepherd boy was not easy in those days. The mornings in the dry season were almost at freezing points, and grazing fields were very far off during those periods. One could wander off for days to find fertile feeding grounds for cattle. Another danger came from wild animals and brigands. Many stories recounted how shepherd boys were often attacked or killed by wild animals or bandits. I am glad my mother, aunts, and uncles were there to talk my father out of his decision. I still did not lose hope three months into the school year but finally lost hope of ever going to school again.

One day, while my mother and I were sitting around the fire in her kitchen, my father paid us a surprise visit. He was careful this time not to propose anything that would further infuriate my mother about me and my future. He told my mother and me that he had found a solution. I was to go to Bamenda and work as a servant to a businessman for five years. According to the agreement, I would be given a shop as a settlement after these five years. I had to leave for Bamenda as soon as possible. It was good news, at least. It brought light and life to our hearts and souls. My mother was particularly overjoyed. Anxiety kept me from sleeping that night. I had never been to the city. I kept wondering what the city looked like, what my new boss might be like, what would become of me in the city, how I would survive without my mother and family, and who the people I would meet were. These questions and many more streamed through my mind. The next day, I broke the news to my friends around our neighbourhood. I saw envy on their faces, and I felt lucky I was leaving the village for the city, where I would work and eventually become rich. I later learned that my boss was a Nigerian businessman, a dealer in building materials named Mr.

Esi Okafor.

Packing my bag for the journey was easy because I did not have many clothes. The best clothes I had were my school uniform. It did not matter much to me then that I lacked many clothes because I kept telling myself I would soon have many boxes full of them. Leaving home was all I could think about until the moment came for the final departure. Parting was bittersweet. Sweet because I was happy to leave for the city, but the thought of leaving my friends, family, and especially my parents brought sadness and tears. They were the people I had known all my life, so how would I survive without their love and warmth? But again, I had to leave if I wanted to help them and put smiles on their faces soon. I was the hope of the family and the sacrificial lamb, so I accepted my father's decision to work in the city partly because I wanted to go, even though I did not know what would become of me. Moreover, God's command to children is to "Respect your parents in words and deeds and serve them as if you were their slave so that you may receive their blessings" (Sir. 3:1-16).

As is customary for children leaving home for foreign lands, I received blessings from my parents the night before my departure. I knelt before them as they prayed for me, spat on my head, and rubbed spittle on my chest. This ritual was supposed to protect me and bring me good luck. Then, all my brothers and sisters took turns wishing me well. That same night, before my departure, I had to leave behind my old clothes because it was hoped and believed that I would get plenty. It was sad to see how my brothers fought over my old dresses. Tears flowed down my cheeks, and I promised to look after them very soon. My sister had nothing because she could not wear my clothes, which made me even sadder.

On the day of my departure, I woke up early because anxiety kept me from sleeping. Before my father knocked twice on our door, I was already there to open it. I ran to my stepmother's doors, knocking on one after the other to bid them farewell. They all gave me their blessings, and one of my stepmothers gave me FCFA 25 to buy something for myself on the way. She was physically challenged; she was an amputee. I was so happy and prayed that God, in His infinite mercy, would keep her safe and always comfort her. I also prayed that one day, God would grant me the grace to touch her life and the lives of many in her condition.

Chapter III - Our Departure to Bamenda

On Friday morning, July 3, 1981, my father and I left Wum for Bamenda. Throughout the journey, expectations and unanswered questions crowded my mind. I wondered if things would work out as my father and new master had promised. What if this business tycoon I would be working for was a cultist or involved in money rituals? What would become of me? Would he make me his slave forever? How were my mother and brothers coping with my absence? Would my mother survive the shock if something terrible happened to me? Would I ever see my family again? These questions and more kept me worried throughout the journey.

When we arrived in Bamenda, my grandfather's reassuring words came to mind. I felt his presence, blessings, and guidance with just the thought of him. Every time I thought of him, I felt as if he were standing next to me. This always had a soothing effect on my spirit and worries.

The journey left me tired and worn out. We travelled in the heart of the rainy season when the road from Wum to Bamenda was at its worst. The 70-kilometre distance that we could cover in at most an hour and a half was taken by the fastest and strongest cars in at least five hours during the rainy season. Certain vehicles even took days to complete the journey. A major characteristic of the Wum-Bamenda stretch of road during this season is the thick, slippery mud, making it almost impossible for a car to go a kilometre without passengers alighting to push the car. We walked half of the journey, which lasted almost eight hours. We set off at 8:00 a.m. and arrived in Bamenda after 8:00 p.m. I was hungry, dirty, and exhausted when we arrived. All I wanted was to eat, bathe, and sleep. Thank God my father understood this quickly. He took me to a small restaurant at the motor park and told me to eat whatever I wanted.

"Eat whatever you wish," he said. "Get something sweet to drink. I know you must be hungry," he concluded.

I did as he said.

My father was one of the good people I have known in my life, someone I will always be grateful to for his kindness. He was a peaceful man, ready to apologize whenever he wronged someone, very hospitable and generous to people—one of the reasons for his material poverty. His respect for others and their views, especially those of children, baffles me. He planned our future with us and was responsible and completely trustworthy. He was my lifeline, and I could write about him and his deeds throughout this book. He was a uniting force for his children and a symbol of genuine love. When we, his grown-up children, were tender and around fifteen, many people expected to see us fighting among ourselves because we were many and from different mothers.

Fortunately, the aforementioned never happened. Our father showed us love and preached the importance and strength of unity, which are the characteristics of our family today. According to the customs and traditions of my people, each woman has to provide food for her husband every day. Five dishes came each day from his five wives. After eating in our kitchens, we would still go to his sitting room and eat from the other dishes. He never asked us why we came to eat with him after dining in our different kitchens. He was a good man and father.

Sometimes, ten of his children would be seen eating from the same dish with him. These were his happiest moments. As I ate, I wondered if I would find the likes of my father (signs of the fear of the Almighty God) in my new boss and master.

For the first time, I saw many people in one place without an occasion or gathering, along with many cars and busy people. I heard different languages and saw tarred roads, storey buildings, and streetlights, to name a few. Bamenda was, indeed, a city, and I was happy to be there. I had come to the city where my father always went for his family allowance and pension, which was short-lived, and where he always bought us bread on his way back to the village.

As we walked from the Ntarinkon Motor Park to my boss's business place, where I would be working, he pointed out a few places and offices he knew and told me their names. As we walked, he reminded me of the few pieces of advice he had given me on the bus along the Wum-Bamenda stretch and what he had told me before we embarked on the journey.

"If you fail, my son," he said, "that will be the end for you and the family. I will be disgraced, and you will suffer. Do not forget how stressful it will be for your mother and me. Follow and respect your master's instructions, and never allow yourself to be tempted by his wealth or touch it. Stay away from women because they can ruin your life in an instant. Avoid bad friends and be open to learning so that after your apprenticeship, you will excel in your business. Your boss will test your loyalty in areas like money, food, and women. You must be vigilant and careful, and be true to yourself. If you are cautious about women, money, and friends, there is no doubt that you will be a successful person soon."

I listened keenly, with my small bag slung over my shoulder. My father continued, "Once you win the trust of such a rich person, you will have won his heart, and your success is guaranteed. But once he distrusts you, you are a prisoner and a failure," he concluded. The last sentence my father used while we were walking to my boss's place was the last thing I wished for myself and for him. I promised him that I would do my best, by the grace of God, not to disappoint him, the family, and myself. I begged him to join my mother in praying for me always. I needed their sincere prayers to see me through.

After walking for about twenty-five to thirty minutes, we finally arrived at my master's shop and my future workplace on Commercial Avenue in Bamenda, opposite the Bamenda Main Market. As we approached the shop, some people sitting there recognized my father. We met five people at the shop, and the oldest, whom I mistook for the boss, greeted my father. My father told me that the person who welcomed us was the manager of my master's business. I did not recognize any of the five people I met at the shop. I observed them carefully, and only one looked cheerful. The rest appeared like battered slaves. I thought they could not remember the last time they were happy, so I felt pity for them.

While I observed the new environment, my father chatted briefly and privately with the manager. When they finished, the manager pulled open a drawer, removed an envelope, and handed it to my father. My father received the envelope with both hands, almost kneeling. It was debasing and embarrassing for me. He thanked him for about five minutes as if he had been given the world. I felt bad and ashamed of myself. If I didn't already know about my father's humility, which felt exaggerated in this case, I would have thought he had sold me to this man.

My father stayed briefly at the shop and finally said he was returning to the village. He held my hand, pulled me to his chest, and wished me goodbye. As I watched him leave, a pang of pain surged in my heart. It felt as if I was losing someone important in my life—the one person

I looked up to for strength and comfort. Tears filled my eyes and blurred my view. I was already missing him, losing the one person I always relied on during troubled times. That was too much! Then I cried. The fears I had while we were in the car to Bamenda resurfaced.

What bothered me was whether I would ever meet my father again, and if so, when? It then occurred to me that my father would not come back to Bamenda again for his pension and family allowance. The government had placed some draconian conditions on pensions and family allowances. The process required a lot of documentation, which my father did not have and could not afford. So, he abandoned everything and stopped coming to Bamenda.

A voice interrupted my thoughts. It was the manager's voice, ordering one of the boys to attend to a customer. About an hour after my father left, no one spoke to or paid attention to me. I thought they might be busy serving other customers. So, I joined one of the cheerful-looking boys who was packing goods into cartons for customers. He showed me how to do it, and I picked it up from there.

My master was one of the biggest traders in Bamenda at that time, specializing in hardware building materials. His shop was so large that it took me three years to gain a proper mastery of the prices and items available. The experience was tough for me; my success and survival depended on it. My first task was to learn how to receive and treat customers, which was not very difficult due to my upbringing. I learned from the boys with whom I worked. They had been there before me and knew every item and its price by heart. I often found myself imagining how long it had taken them to master all this knowledge and what agreement they had with the master. They could tell the position of every item even with their eyes closed. Our shop had an influx of customers daily, allowing me to learn quickly.

Before my father returned to the village from Bamenda, he told me that an agreement regarding my stay with my boss had not yet been reached and that a conclusion would only be finalized when my master returned from his trip to Nigeria.

On my first day at the shop, it was about 7:30 p.m. when the manager ordered us to start packing things up. As we were closing the shop, he turned to me and asked, "What is your name?"

"Geh Kum," I replied. He introduced himself to me and the others, briefly explaining what the business was all about. He also told me that the master had many other shops around town, but that the one we were in was the biggest and the main shop. He outlined what was expected of me, and one person was assigned to train me for my incorporation. I later learned that his name was Uche. He was to teach me the names and prices of goods. He was a good-looking guy, and I was happy to have him as my teacher.

The manager was worried about me. I was small in size, and he did not think I could lift half of the goods in the shop. That was probably because he had never seen me in the village and did not know what I could do, carrying heavier objects than myself. Anyway, I still had to prove myself to him, which I eventually did. He ended by telling the four boys that I was answerable to all of them, but particularly to Uche. They were happy to have a younger apprentice in their midst, partly because it would take some burdens off their shoulders and because they could finally have someone younger to run their errands and push around. I saw them whispering to each other when this announcement was made.

While we were packing up, more customers kept coming, and the drawers were filled with money. This was my first time seeing such an amount of money. It bothered me why some people were so rich while others, like my parents, were so poor. Why did my village work so hard yet remain so impoverished? Life seemed unfair to many. I was determined to work hard and break the yoke of poverty in my family lineage.

When the last item was packed into the store and we were waiting for the shop doors to be closed, everyone gathered around the cashier to count the money for the day. I saw piles of banknotes I had never imagined. My mouth remained partly open for a long time at what I saw. The sales for that day totalled more than a million CFA francs. That was in 1981. I could not express what I was seeing; it felt strange to me. That amount was more than my father's income for three years. It was then that I understood why my father almost worshipped Mr. Esi Okafor, my master, and why he nearly knelt to receive the envelope handed to him earlier that day by the manager.

I wondered what the total daily sales were. After we all finished counting the money for the day, the manager announced that two hundred CFA francs (200) were missing from the total. I was surprised. Why would this happen only on my first day at the shop? Or was this always the case? Fear, confusion, and shame gripped me. Before I knew it, the manager picked up a saw blade from the table and struck the cashier with it so hard that it left traces of blood on his forehead. My fear of the place increased, and my blood ran cold. How would I survive? Would I cope? My fear intensified, and I hated the place instantly with every fibre of my being.

"How did this happen?" he snarled. "I have always told you that if this happens again, I will send you packing to your parents," he continued. He pulled the boy out from behind the counter, searched his pockets, and slapped him. "Explain, you fool, or you will suffer for this!" he shouted.

When all this was taking place, one of the boys was busy cross-checking the register. He later discovered, as God would have it, that there was a miscalculation. He warned again that if this happened, we would regret it for the rest of our lives. It was a threat. He angrily and unapologetically sent us off to the house. I pitied the cashier. I later learned his name was Uche. It was the most dreadful scene I had ever witnessed in my life. It paralyzed my emotions and marred the anxiety with which I had come to serve my master. I now realized why the boys looked so dirty, sickly, skinny, and unkempt when I had seen them earlier in the day. That night, my grandfather's words ran through my mind: "You will go through many rotten bridges, but I will always be there to assist you. Prison awaits you if you bring us disgrace and stress..." These words reassured me. But if I had known any family member residing in Bamenda, I would have run to them that same night.

My new home was on Savanah Hotel Street, Big Mankon. After leaving the shop on my first day, we got home at 8:30 p.m. To my greatest dismay, the place where I would spend most of my life was not at all what I had anticipated. It was dirty and deplorable. Ten boys lived in two rooms with bunk beds on either side. It was a stuffy dormitory with a space smaller than our master's sitting room. I felt cheated, rejected, deceived, and, worse, like an outcast. I thought of the stories I had heard about the suffering of Black Americans and the struggles of Martin Luther King Jr., who, because of his family's middle-class standing, was more fortunate than most other Black children. Yet economic well-being could not change the social stigma against African Americans in a country where the white majority belittled and discriminated against people of colour.

I thought of how segregationists used their financial power to keep Black people in a permanently subordinate position in American society. I pictured myself living the same scenario. That night was a dark one for me. I could not bring myself to sleep. I was worried and frightened, feeling hopeless and helpless. I recalled the incident that had taken place at the shop earlier that day over and over again. If the manager could behave in such a mean manner, what would the master's attitude be like? Would he be any different? This question remained unanswered. I wanted to blame God for cursing the Black race with so much pain, hatred, and suffering. If Esi Okafor were going to be like Che, the manager, then life would be a living hell for me.

I also discovered that same night that we were only boys with no mother or woman around to cook for us. Despite the tedious day's work and our fatigue, the boys entered the kitchen that night to prepare what we would eat. The kitchen was an attachment to the house, and we used firewood to cook. As the boys cooked, they chatted freely and happily because no one was around to reprimand them. They discussed the events of the day, made jokes, and commented on various topics. It was a relaxing and relieving moment for them. From their discussions, I learned a bit about my master.

"If patron bi dey there when that tin happens, something terrible for happen," one of the boys said.

I then questioned them, "Where patron yi madam dey?"

"Madam no dey stay here. She dey do business for Nigeria, and she fit come here one time in many years," Uche, one of the boys, answered. "Na because oga want to be going after small Cameroonian girls weh make him leave madam for Nigeria," another added, and they all laughed.

I could not comprehend what I heard about my master, but it seemed all too true. I was in another world, different from the village setting from which I came. The village was calm, as almost everyone there lived in harmony with their neighbours, unlike what was taking place in the city. Life seemed to move faster in the city than in the village. The boys in the shop found happiness in talking about the manager and the master, as that was the only way they could find solace after a tedious day's work.

I found it terrible that a man like Mr. Esi Okafor would leave his wife in another country just to chase after young girls. It was satanic, debasing, and abnormal, and I instantly decided to be vigilant. It was my first day in the city. That night, we finally went to bed at 11:30. Before going to sleep, Uche informed me we would have to be up as early as 5:30 a.m. to prepare for work.

The next day was a Saturday, specifically the 4th of July, 1981. As I had been informed the night before, the day began at 5:30 a.m. In Bamenda during those days, Saturday was the Main Market Day when people from nearby towns and villages came to sell their products. As I had been told and later discovered, many customers visited the shop that morning, and the streets were crowded. It was my first Saturday at work, so I asked Uche if the town was always this busy. He explained why it was so. I hoped to meet someone from my tribe, as Uche had mentioned that people came from far and nearby villages to trade and buy goods on Saturdays. To my disappointment, I didn't see anyone from my village. I finally had my interview with the manager, Che, that same day.

It was more of an interrogation or first contact than an interview. He asked questions about me and my family. There was no hint of humour in his tone, and he wore a stern expression throughout. I was partly terrified because of what I had seen him do to the cashier the day before and also because of what I had learned about him from the boys the previous night. I chose my words carefully and watched my tongue as if any misplaced word might provoke his anger. His questions kept coming until a customer arrived whom I had to assist, finally rescuing me. It was a narrow escape and a relief. Whenever I got closer to Che, he asked a question that made me panic. I therefore decided to avoid being near him that day.

That Saturday afternoon, I accompanied one of the boys to the Bamenda

Food Market to buy foodstuff for the house. It was to help me get acquainted with the market since, being the youngest, I was expected to run errands. I later found out that his name was Suh. It was the largest market I had ever seen. In the village, our markets were small. I saw many Nigerians and Bamilekés, and I soon discovered that they were the economic giants of Bamenda. As Suh and I walked through the market, I received more disheartening and stunning revelations about my new home. Suh told me that each of the eight of us was entitled to FCFA 100 a day for food. The only meal that was affordable and substantial enough for that amount was rice. For the past three years he had spent with the master, they had eaten only rice. He further shocked me by adding that they were not allowed to eat meat at home and that before cooking, the cook counted the meat, and only the master ate it. How could the master be so wealthy, yet his workers live in such poverty? I was determined to find the answers.

My third day in Bamenda was a Sunday. My parents were Christians, and they taught us that church doctrine was essential; we were never allowed to miss church service for any reason. My mother made sure we went to church every Sunday. My first Sunday in Bamenda was the 5th of July, 1981. I realized that on Sundays, everyone was encouraged to go to church. The boys were excited because it allowed them to visit their relatives and catch a brief break from the tense home environment. My master encouraged the boys to attend church so that the church and the word of God would prick our consciences and make us not steal from him. Though we could go to church, we had to return home ten minutes after the service ended. We were all from different denominations: Catholics, Presbyterians, and Baptists. I joined the group who worshipped at the Presbyterian Church at Ntamulung, Bamenda. Church service always began at 9:00 a.m., and I was glad to continue fellowshipping in Bamenda.

Sundays were typically manual labour and general clean-up days—from splitting wood and cooking to washing clothes and tidying up the place. Che, the manager, would always come to the house unannounced to check if we were home, respected the day's schedule, and ensured everything was in order. We were not allowed to have friends, especially of the opposite sex, for fear that the girls might influence us to start stealing from the master. I found these rules surprising. In my village, I was allowed to make as many friends as I wished. This restriction felt like punishment; how could one live without friends?

I couldn't connect with most of the boys I knew as I had told them about life in the village. None of it seemed to make sense to them. They just laughed and said, "wait and see." Each time they told me anything, I seemed surprised, and they laughed at me. Time, indeed, would become the agent revealing all the events of that period. That evening, the older boys sneaked out of the house, saying they had things to do in town and weren't slaves. Although they dreaded the master's anger if he found out, they still took the risk, especially when he was away on business in Nigeria. They would not dare if he were around. I stayed at home, unable to summon the courage to do the same.

I considered Monday, July 6, 1981, the beginning of my journey into the business world. My training started quickly. I began learning the different names of our products, their prices, and each item's code. They taught me how to make entries, and I also polished my skills in welcoming, receiving, and attending to customers. Convincing a customer to buy our goods was one of my strong points, and each time I succeeded, I prided myself on my skill, adding an imaginary red feather to my cap. I was determined to do my best and leave the rest to our Maker. Yet, I couldn't ignore the poor treatment Manager Che gave the boys, which kept me constantly on guard.

I thought, "If Che could be that harsh to the boys, then the master might be even worse." That thought kept coming back to me. Each time I felt discouraged and downcast, my grandfather's words returned to me: "…you will cross many dangling bridges to become a great man in this life…I will always keep my eyes on you and hold you up whenever you fall." I thought of the five years of apprenticeship ahead and wondered if I would make it through to the end. But I had to; I had promised my father, brothers, and sisters that I would return for them. I had also vowed to break every barrier to see my family rise. I owed it to them—and to myself—to succeed. If others could and had done it, why should it be different for me? I was determined to overcome every challenge on my path to success.

Chapter IV - The Return of Mr. Esi Okafor

It was a cold night two weeks after I had arrived in Bamenda. Late that night, we heard a violent and continuous knock on the door, sending chills down our spines. This was the master's characteristic way of knocking. My master, Mr. Esi Okafor, was back. Panic set in as we debated who would open the door for him. Outside, we could hear him shouting our names. "You sleep like corpses," he snarled. When the door finally opened, he pushed his way in and, without any further formalities, bombarded us with questions. His eyes scanned every corner of our dormitory, inspecting to see that everything was in order. The boys, still half-asleep, took turns explaining all that had transpired in his absence.

Mr. Okafor was a tall, dark-skinned man with a deep baritone voice and an imposing presence. He wasn't the all-smiling type; rather, he was a "no-nonsense" person. His main concern was the manager's financial transactions while he was away and the balance in his bank account. After the boys had explained everything, he turned to me and gave a rare I'm-happy-to-see-you smile. He asked if I could manage the job at the shop. I briefed him on my activities over the past two weeks and my work in the village. My competence seemed to reassure him, and he was visibly satisfied. I wasn't sure where I found the courage to speak so confidently, but I did, and his last words were, "You are an intelligent boy."

Throughout our discussion, I noticed he spoke typical Nigerian Pidgin English, something I was hearing up close for the first time. There were moments I was tempted to laugh, but I dared not, knowing the potential consequences. He left our dormitory at 2:30 a.m. After he was gone, Uche advised me to be careful with the boys, warning that one of them was an informant for the master, reporting everything that happened in his absence. He cautioned me to be wary of everyone. The night felt short, as we were up by 5:30 a.m. to open the shop by 6:30 a.m.

My stay with Mr. Esi Okafor taught me the meaning of "rotten" and "dangling bridges," phrases that, until then, had made no sense to me. The pressure of being his servant was immense, yet I had to bear it to bring light to my family. I had given up my education and family life for this. It dawned on me that to succeed in this mission, I needed more than courage. I needed to adopt a lifestyle that would carry me through. Eventually, I settled on humility, focus, obedience, discretion, faith, and prayer.

Above all, I chose to believe in myself, as Norman Peale says: "Believe in yourself, and all will work out for you." I knew it wouldn't be easy. Adopting a new way of life was challenging. Each morning before leaving for the shop, we cleaned the surroundings and prepared breakfast for the master—a breakfast we never had ourselves. We were only given lunch and supper. And we were expected to be at the shop by 6:30 a.m.; failing to do so meant a day full of insults and punishment. It was hard for me, so different from life back home, where I was cared for and could do as I pleased.

I put immense effort into learning from my master's business each day. I was a servant, and I did my best to remain in that position. I was poor and needed wealthy people like Mr. Esi Okafor to help break the chains of poverty, though he, too, needed the poor, like myself, to make him richer. He never understood this way of thinking. His presence in the shop was a constant threat to all of us. Whenever he was around, he would be either threatening, shouting abusive words, or even slapping and kicking some of us. He trusted no one when it came to money. He worshipped money.

Money was like a god to Mr. Okafor. He took a particular interest in me because I worked hard, gave my all, and was the youngest. He feared the older boys might corrupt my young mind, so he often advised me to embrace suffering and endure what I was going through, saying it was preparing me for a brighter, better future. He also told me to steer clear of women. Just like my father, he believed that women posed the greatest danger and hindrance to a young business person's success. While I understood his point, I also knew it was rooted in his fear that I might start stealing his money to spend on women and young girls. He was securing his money and nothing more.

My quick learning and dedication to understanding the business led to my promotion to cashier in November 1982—evidence of trust and confidence in me. But why was I chosen over older boys who had been there longer? I saw it as both a blessing and a potential trap. On the one hand, I would no longer be carrying heavy items or running errands for the other boys; on the other hand, any issue with the finances could be blamed on me, especially since my master had an unusual fondness for me. The other boys could easily frame me. However, God was always by my side, and I kept the records clean and up-to-date. My master consistently praised me for maintaining spotless financial records.

I worked under constant fear, as each year, he dismissed salespeople over minor, sometimes insignificant, issues. Even rumours of having a girlfriend could result in immediate termination, which happened to many who left. I worried often about how my friends and colleagues left the shop. Their departures brought setbacks to Mr. Esi Okafor's business and left their families in difficult situations. Many salespeople, after dedicating three, four, or even five years to the shop, found themselves jobless with little to survive on. Mr. Okafor's actions strained many families and discouraged some of us from giving our best. His love for wealth drove him to exploit countless innocent children.

My master's attitude disheartened and terrified me. What if I were the next to be dismissed unceremoniously? It would destroy me. I turned to God, in whom I put all my trust. I was confident that He would see me through. To me, Mr. Esi Okafor represented injustice, exploitation, and cruelty. I feared for him, as the Bible warns about the love of money. It clearly states that the love of money is "a trap that every fool will fall into," causing worry, sleepless nights, and ultimately, torment (Sirach 31:1-8). The love of money is the root of all kinds of evil (1

Tim. 6). Children of the light must put God before everything (Mt 6:24-30), as this perishable world will pass along with its riches, but the Word of God will endure forever (1 Jn 2:15-17).

"What gain will be yours if you gain the whole world but lose your soul in hell?"

I wondered if Mr. Esi Okafor ever read the Bible and considered these truths. What did he take away from his Sunday Masses? I pitied him, as he seemed destined for hell unless he repented from his love of money and cruelty (Rev. 21:5-8). I feared the disastrous consequences awaiting the wicked, hypocrites, and unjust, which kept me constantly on guard. The sins of the unjust block their prayers, for the God of justice does not listen to the cries of the unjust (Is. 59:1-3). My master was the architect of his own suffering due to his exploitation, enslavement, and the downfall of so many young people whom he unjustly dismissed each time they were nearing their due settlement.

As the years passed, the master-servant relationship deteriorated steadily. Wickedness, enslavement, conspiracy, and hypocrisy became the order of the day, even among us, the servants and salesboys. Just as Uche had warned me before the day my master returned from his trip to Nigeria, I met him for the first time. Uche had told me about a "black-legged" among us who regularly updated the master on our activities. These individuals provided false reports to gain favour with the master, a practice especially common among Nigerian salesboys. This behaviour created a divide between the Cameroonian and Nigerian salesboys.

One thing my master despised about me was my quiet nature and my refusal to bring him information about a fellow worker. He constantly accused me of conspiring with the others to steal from him, often threatening me. I never reported anything to him because I didn't know of any wrongdoing. I saw no benefit in tarnishing the reputation of a fellow brother for personal gain. I couldn't bring myself to do that—I consider it satanic, though it's all too common in workplaces today. It's an age-old phenomenon. Many have risen from gatekeepers to managers through gossip and lies about their colleagues. Some even go as far as visiting witch doctors for charms to gain favour with their bosses. But those who reach the top through deceit often meet a drastic downfall. What the devil grants never lasts for eternity; it brings untold sorrow in the end. When the unjustly treated cry out to the Lord for justice, the wicked will flee.

Scriptures remind us, "The prayers of a humble person pierce the clouds into heaven… he will not stop until the Most High hears and looks down until justice is rendered in favour of the righteous" (Sir. 35:17-18). This message is clear: those who oppress the upright will face divine justice when the Almighty comes to defend the wronged. The Egyptians, Sodom and Gomorrah, those in Noah's time, and others are proof of the Lord's vengeance. Many households cried out against Mr. Esi Okafor and his company; he had treated many of his workers unjustly. I thought of how God dealt with Cain when Abel's blood cried for vengeance—God cursed Cain (Gen. 4:10-16). I was fading under the weight of the injustices dealt to those repeatedly dismissed. No one could challenge the master. I turned to prayer. I noticed something unusual happened each time I prayed earnestly: the wicked boys who fabricated stories to cost others their jobs all eventually faced serious trouble. They were either caught red-handed squandering money in bars, impregnating young schoolgirls—causing scandal and involvement with the gendarmes—or caught outrightly stealing.

These incidents always led them to the brigade or police stations, where they faced harsh treatment from gendarmes and police. All this felt biblical: "Whatever you do in darkness will come to light, for nothing is hidden from the eyes of God Almighty." I witnessed God's saving power in action, and I trusted that as long as I remained truthful and innocent, no harm would come my way. No matter how long we endure injustice, joy will follow when God's justice arrives. The Book of Wisdom tells us, "The souls of the just are in the hands of the Lord, and no torment shall befall them. Yet the wicked feel they have lost everything" (Wisdom 3:1-6).

On May 23, 1983, I was promoted to company cashier—a delicate and tempting role. The year prior, three people had been dismissed for embezzlement or mismanagement. That same year, we lost two colleagues, Eze and Joseph, during an unannounced dormitory search. The master found eight thousand francs (FCFA 8000) and incriminating love letters in their trunks. They were dismissed that night with no compensation, despite Eze having worked for three years and Joseph for four. Those years were wasted, and their departure left us with a heavier workload.

The following years were challenging. I was responsible for the company's funds, customer service, and record-keeping for over forty tonnes of goods from Douala and Nigeria. It was overwhelming. Some days, my master would slap me for minor mistakes; other days, I'd go to work with a swollen eye from the previous day's punishment. We'd spend entire days offloading building materials from trucks, return home at 7:00 p.m., and start cooking dinner. Often, we were too exhausted to eat; we'd sit on the bed to rest after cooking, only to wake up at 5:30 a.m., readying ourselves for another day.

The thought of lifting my family out of poverty kept me going. I wasn't going to give up on my parents or myself. I was determined to see it through to the end.

No matter how dark the night, it must eventually give way to day. There were times when I thought the suffering and persecution would never end. Yet, I knew deep down that, despite everything, there would be light at the end of the tunnel for me and my family. Blaming others is easy. Even though Mr. Esi Okafor was as he was, not all he said was senseless. At times, he shared truths that could genuinely help a business flourish. The problem was his extremes—his insatiable appetite and love for money, which drove him to hurt others. One truth he told us, as aspiring business people, was that every franc leaving the business unaccounted for would eventually ruin the enterprise, and this was true. In those days, it wasn't uncommon to see big businesses collapsing daily due to mismanagement and the misappropriation of funds.

Some salespeople or servants were extravagant, and they ruined many successful businesses. It was common to see salesboys squandering money in bars and nightclubs with young women, some even housing them, paying their fees, and sponsoring their families entirely. It was a pitiful sight. If one cannot manage another's business well, how can he hope to manage his own when the time comes? So, I remained focused, treating my master's business as if it were my own. There are both good and bad masters, just as there are good and bad servants. We must rely on and trust in God for everything.

Every incident around me became a lesson, drawing me closer to God, in whom I found solace and comfort. I prayed daily to stay faithful to Mr. Esi Okafor, no matter what happened. My conscience was always my greatest judge, and I was often shocked by the hardened consciences of others. To think a man could cheat, embezzle, or even harm another human being was difficult to comprehend. I learned not to judge because judgment itself is sinful. Humans are weak, and we need God's grace and mercy to make us strong. So, I continued to trust the Lord for my perfection, and that kept me going. Without God, we can do nothing (John 15:5). It is written, "If God does not build and protect the city, it is in vain that the builder and guards do their work" (Ps.127:1).

Chapter V - My Spiritual Engagement

Our mother instilled in us a deep love for God from the time we were born. She ensured that, under her watchful eye, we would not stray from Him. Though she could neither read nor write, God blessed her with the wisdom to know and revere Him. She constantly watched over us, ensuring we never missed a church program. Through her care and encouragement, a commitment to God became part and parcel of our lives. My mother always reminded us that the only way to overcome and defeat the devil was through the Bible and the Word of God.

When I came to Bamenda, however, things changed. My spiritual life began to falter without anyone to guide me, coupled with the demanding workload I faced daily. One day, I realized I was not fully living out the Christian values my mother and upbringing had instilled in me. I felt a twinge of guilt and resolved to rekindle the zeal and passion with which I had followed and loved the things of God back home.

There was an unsettling and suspicious feeling surrounding the activities and life of Mr. Esi Okafor. The only way to find peace and clarity was to trust in God and seek a closer relationship with Him. My first prayer was for God to give me a renewed desire for Him. My second was for Him to touch Mr. Esi Okafor's heart. I deepened my spirituality by engaging more actively in church activities at the Presbyterian Church Ntamulung, under the guidance of Rev. Pastor Perfock. Each time I attended church, I felt lighter and more renewed. Jesus promises us rest in Matthew 11:28: "Come to me, all you who carry heavy burdens, and I will give you rest." The Sunday messages, worship, and praise songs uplifted my soul.

Soon, my colleagues began noticing the positive changes my renewed engagement with God brought into my life. Each day, I faced life with newfound strength and courage.

I joined the Young Presbyterians and became an active member. We often challenged Catholics for their perceived ignorance of the Scriptures. One aspect that angered us was their reverence for Mary. To us, it seemed as though they worshipped her, which was unacceptable to our faith. We grew tired of their prayers of "Hail Mary…" and "Our Father" every time a Catholic was called to pray. They excelled at memorizing and reciting these prayers, but when asked to share a reflection, they became tongue-tied. Presbyterians were concerned about the salvation of Catholics, but I later realized that salvation is not merely about knowledge of the Scriptures or how well we can speak in public; it is about doing God's will. Saint Paul teaches in 1 Corinthians 13:1-9 that speaking like an angel without true love does one no good. Mastering the Scriptures does not make one a better Christian. Many Christians continue to make the mistake of limiting the reign of God to the memorization of a few biblical passages. Jesus is not only the Christ of the Scriptures but also the Christ of apostolic tradition and practices that align with the reign of heaven. God's ways differ from our ways, and His command is final (Isaiah 55:9-11).

Church and life within the church were sweet, especially when I made Jesus my best friend. He was easy to talk to, and I could reach out to Him anytime and anywhere. Having a good relationship with Christ was far better than making friends with people. I trusted Jesus (Sirach 6:15-17; Psalm 118). During the Apartheid regime in South Africa and the fight for Black liberation in America, the only thing that provided hope and aided in their ultimate freedom was their reliance on God for everything, finding peace and joy in His presence. That is why, through God's love and intervention, preachers and pastors like Rev. Dr. Martin Luther King Jr. championed the fight for Negro freedom and liberty. Despite being beaten, tortured, enslaved, and oppressed, they put their trust in the Lord through His servants and inspired leaders like Moses, who led the Israelites to liberation from the cruel hands of the Egyptians.

It was even more painful to see someone like Mr. Esi Okafor, a fellow Black person, treat us as if we were worthless. We could not eat meat, even when our families visited and brought him goats and fowls. We could not stay after church for more than ten minutes,

My spiritual engagement

nor could we have friends, male or female. We ate once or sometimes twice a day and were not allowed to visit family members. He restricted us to the point that we felt worse than slaves and prisoners, as our liberty had been confiscated.

Mr Esi Okafor preached virtue but practised vice. Every virtuous person and a good leader must be ready to practice what they preach as an example for their followers. Many servants lost their jobs for having female friends. My master was no different from those servants and salespeople he dismissed. He was the worst; though he was a married man, he kept many women, especially students, and spent large sums of money on them. As the cashier, I sometimes wrote letters on his behalf, enclosing substantial amounts of money for young girls. It was shameful to see my once-respected and strict businessman fall so low.

To succeed in business, one must maintain good relationships with those who support it and respect those who help keep it running. He misplaced his charity and mistreated those he was supposed to motivate. I saw his lavish expenditures on young girls as a punishment for his wrongdoings. Nemesis was catching up to him. There were many poor and needy people around him he could have helped, but he closed his eyes and heart to their plight. God rewards those who are charitable to the poor (Sirach 35:1-10). I considered all he did to be vanity with no reward, as outlined in the Book of Ecclesiastes (1:2, 2:8-11), which says, "Vanity of vanities, all is vanity. What profit is there for a man in all his work which he toils under the sun? I acquired silver and gold, the wealth of kings and nations, and all pleasures. Then I considered all I had achieved by my work and all the toil it had entailed and found that it was senseless, a chasing after the wind. There is no profit under the sun."

Mr. Esi Okafor is one of those few who, I believe, does not believe that heaven is real; those who think there is no afterlife. It is a monumental error for any human being to live as if there is no God. There is a God, and He exists. The afterlife is a reality, and to enjoy it with God and all His heavenly hosts, we must fear, obey, praise, and revere Him. The Bible tells us that the fear of God is the beginning of wisdom. How can we, therefore, be truly wise if we do not believe in His word? Riches and evil do not provide security; only a just and humble life does. Sirach 31:5-8 further tells us that no one who loves wealth can be righteous. The love of wealth has ruined many; it is a trap for the foolish. That is why Matthew 6:24 tells us that one cannot serve both God and money. We cannot serve two masters at the same time. The rich man Jesus spoke of in the Bible could not be His disciple because he could not give up his riches for the kingdom of heaven. I prayed that I would never abandon the Lord for any reason—abandoning God is like building on sandy ground.

I stood firm in my service to God with all my might, mind, body, and soul under Mr. Esi Okafor. I had to ensure my faith was rooted in Jesus Christ. It would be a shame to abandon or show little concern for the one true God, whom my mother taught me to trust. Although my mother could neither read nor write, she loved the Word and never failed to hear it read to her. She could quote some scriptural passages and always did her best to retain what the pastors said in church. Her zeal for the things of God was evident in the early baptisms she arranged for all her children. All her children were baptized a few months after birth, and she made sure we were constantly committed to the things of God.

As a young Presbyterian, I thought Martin Luther was the pope of the Presbyterian Church until, after some years, I finally understood that it was an independently run church administered by a moderator. I learned much about Martin Luther from my pastors in those days because they spoke extensively about him. I did not hear anything about the positive aspects of the Catholic Church and its authenticity, perhaps because most of the pastors did not know much about the Catholic faith or partly because they did not want to discuss it. Martin Luther was portrayed as the true prophet who redressed and redirected the path of the modern church with his ninety-five (95) theses, which did not give glory to God. The Protestant doctrine taught us a great deal about the effects of the 16th century and how they marked a turning point in the history of Christianity, influenced by Martin Luther.

I was a supporter, crusader, and defender of Martin Luther and the Protestant doctrine. I defended the Protestant church with the same zeal and passion that Paul exhibited with Gamaliel in Judaism. I failed to see and understand that it was one thing to make a name in history and another to handle the consequences of what you did that placed you in the annals of history. History has made great names that were ultimately damaged because they could not successfully manage what they had started, and the consequences were disastrous. When I think of the two World Wars, civil wars, and disorders, and how they brought untold suffering to humanity, the worst and most painful reality is that all the authors and initiators are often sorry for their actions. I wonder if Martin Luther and his followers regret today the division they caused in God's body, and whether he would be proud of the many churches, Protestant groups, or religious movements we find in our communities.

I will never stop thanking my parents for introducing us to the things of God at tender ages. The family is the first church, and my parents ensured that we understood this while instilling the spirit of communal life in us. They taught us the values of sharing and giving, which stood in stark contrast to what I experienced at Mr. Esi Okafor's home. I felt homesick each time I thought of home and how wonderful our family was. Mr. Okafor never allowed his servants to visit their parents during their apprenticeship. I was no exception. He was afraid that his servants would be reminded of their plights each time they saw their families, which might prevent them from returning.

It had been almost five years since I last saw my mother and siblings. My father had visited twice. Each time he came, I was not allowed to talk with him for long. My boss gave my father money and promised to settle me soon by opening a shop for me. My father always returned happy and fulfilled, ignoring my complaints even when I tried to voice them. I attempted to warn him of Mr. Esi Okafor's cunning nature, but he never once listened. He was eager to know when I would be settled and start my own business. I could not wait. It had already been five years, and I was not seeing any signs that my boss would soon open a shop for me. I was worried. I imagined how much my younger brothers and sisters had grown, and nostalgia made me cry. I missed them and everything about them. My boss severed all communication with our parents and guardians. Visits from family members and relatives, apart from our parents, were taboo. He visited his home several times a year.

My father visited in January of 1986 and realized I had grown big and strong. It was so joyful and relieving to see him. He found me in shabby clothes with a bloodshot eye, which raised alarm in his mind. He could not overlook it. That day, Mr. Esi Okafor ensured that I did not have even 10 minutes to spend beside my father for fear that I might spill everything to him. He even made sure that I spent the night in the sitting room to separate me from my father so I would not tell him about the horrible things he did to us. As usual, Mr. Okafor spoke highly of me and promised to pay me off so I could start my business as soon as possible. He even told my father he would adopt me as one of his sons. He claimed that if he was hard on us, it was because he wanted the best for us and to make us mature and hardworking businesspeople in the future; otherwise, the mafia world would draw us in and swallow us. His sweet talk only served to infuriate me further.

I wanted to tell my father that the slavery of the Jews in Egypt was far better than what we were experiencing with my master. He had said nothing concrete about when my work with him would end. Most Nigerian businesspeople hardly signed contracts with their servants or their parents and guardians for fear of any legal action against them in case things did not work out well. I depended on God, not even on my father, to see my case through. I was so glad when my father visited; I could finally get news about my mother, brothers, and sisters. He said they were all doing great. My father looked much younger than I had imagined, but it was also sad to hear that some family members had died.

He told me that Mr. Esi Okafor trusted me greatly and counted on me to maintain the same attitude and not disgrace or tarnish the family name. He expressed confidence that I was going to make it. Then he left Bamenda for the village. Parting from my father, the only family member I had seen and talked to after so many years, was not easy. If only he could stay longer and allow me to explain what I had been going through! Those were mere wishes. He had to go, and he left. For a moment, his departure created a hollow feeling in me, and the memories of his brief visit lingered in my mind for a long time. His presence gave me hope that somewhere in this world, I still had someone who cared for me and believed in me—someone who relied on my patience, hard work, and diligence. I knew and believed that Christ, the way, the truth, and the life, would always see me through.

Chapter VI - I Am Made Manager of A New Branch

In late 1986, Mr Okafor's business had grown, necessitating an expansion into other areas of the neighbourhood. A new branch was, therefore, opened on Ring Way Street, Bamenda. He had three branches in the same town, and the new one was the second largest. I was appointed the new branch manager because I had won the trust and confidence of my master, and I had learned and mastered the business. By the end of 1987, the shop I managed had become the busiest building material shop on the street. I was answerable to the general manager, Che, whom everyone suspected had bewitched the master into only listening to him. He, too, was not an easy nut to crack. Even though I was the branch manager, he treated me with disdain and disrespect. Everything he told the master was final, and he could make decisions independently. The master never thought twice about any proposal that came from him, allowing Che to run the business without any external support or advice. He never consulted his sub-managers on any decision concerning the entire business. My master only wanted to know the profit he had made at the end of each year, which was dangerous for a shrewd businessman like Mr. Esi Okafor. I fought hard to see my branch grow, and before long, the master started taking an interest in me and was amazed at my progress.

My rapid growth and progress became a blessing to Mr. Esi Okafor and a misfortune for me. Che noticed that I was making strides and, thus, winning the master's attention. In his jealousy, he turned against me, marking the beginning of a slippery relationship between us. As the general manager, he supplied us with goods on command. I noticed that each time I requested goods, he would either fail to deliver them or would deliver them late. As fate would have it, the more he did that, the more profit I made, surprisingly to the glory of God. With the help of my collaborator at the time, Ignatius, we built good business relations with many big customers, some of whom were technicians, contractors, and subcontractors, and these people bought in large quantities. One of my most respectable customers was the Nangah and Bongam Companies Ltd. I faced many difficulties with technicians from these companies because they were experts at inflating bills.

They would buy at a lower cost from us and ask us to issue receipts with inflated amounts. This action always bothered me, but I had to do it because I needed to keep my customers. That was how most businesses survived in those days. We struggled, and in December 1988, two years after I was made manager, the general manager and the master decided to audit my stock to ascertain how much profit and progress I had made during that period. After the auditing and stocktaking, they informed my master that I had made a profit of over five million seven hundred thousand (5.7 million) francs CFA. The master was surprised and confused! He saw me as a treasure and then made me a partner in his business. It was a smart move on his part.

He knew I would soon leave, taking some of my customers with me, which would negatively impact his business and profit margin. So, he weighed the possibilities and announced that as his business partner, my shares would be FCFA four hundred thousand (400,000). I had already put in seven to eight years of service to this man. That amount was small compared to the years and profit of over FCFA twenty million (20,000,000) I had generated for him. I was so disappointed because I was expecting far more than that; at least FCFA two million five hundred thousand (2,500,000) to start would have been encouraging. This information shocked my parents, especially my father because it did not match the initial agreement. It confirmed our complaints and opened my eyes to the injustice in this world, where we see the poor slaving to enrich the rich further. After consulting my family, I accepted the offer, hoping to make more profit and build a stronger partnership. I immersed myself more in prayers, hoping and believing that things would soon improve.

I came in as the third partner in the business after Che. They decided that I would receive 20 per cent of the profits made by the company each year.

I could not wait to announce this good news to my parents, which brought much happiness and rejoicing back home. I thanked God for making it possible. It was indeed good news. I immediately set to work and gave my best. However, my new status as a partner was not good news for Che. Becoming a partner in the business meant lower profits for him, and I would have to be involved in any decision-making that affected the entire business. He immediately set to work—ruining and undermining me, and two months into my partnership, he convinced the master to conduct a stocktaking in my shop.

He told the master that he felt the shop was scanty, so it was urgent to conduct an audit to ensure everything was running smoothly. Previously, my master did not consider his allegations because he had total and complete trust in me, but Che kept complaining and pressuring him. Since my master was a money lover, he ultimately gave in to Che's pressure. To see his plans through, the master began complaining that I was already behaving as if I were the master of the company. He menaced me, keeping me under surveillance and monitoring. I became confused, disappointed, discouraged, and depressed.

I started sensing danger in my spirit and soul. I knew it was the manager's handiwork, and I waited for him to do his worst. The Word of the Lord says, "Be sober, be vigilant, for the devil is roaming like a roaring lion looking for someone to devour." I needed to be vigilant; otherwise, I would be devoured. I prayed to the Lord, "Oh God, do not forsake me in the hands of the wicked. Frustrate the plans of my enemies, protect me with your powerful hands, and lead me to my destiny, but may only your will be done. Amen." The feeling of the passion and death of Jesus Christ came over me, and a sharp pain like that from a sword went through my heart. That was an indication that the hour of gloom had come.

In March 1989, less than three months after our partnership, Mr. Esi Okafor ordered that the famous stock audit be conducted—the first of its kind since I was employed. It usually happens after one to two years. He left for a long Easter holiday in Nigeria, only to return after the audit. The stock audit modalities put in place were very complicated. Since I entered the company in 1981, Mr. Che has always done the stock auditing alone, without the assistance of a professional accountant. I wondered how authentic the stock auditing was. Mr. Esi Okafor had given him so much confidence and power that no one could shake him. Many people, especially customers and employees in the company, thought they had used a spell on Mr. Esi Okafor. Anything said against the manager brought enmity between Okafor and the person.

Consequently, we suffered a lot of slavery, frustration, and permanent pressure because he never let anyone excel in the company. He did everything to blackmail Mr. Esi Okafor against anyone who attracted his attention. We later realized why my boss loved him so much: though very rich, he could barely read and write. Eventually, this famous stock audit was catastrophic. My feelings of disaster came true; it resulted in a deficit of FCFA one million nine thousand (1,009,000 FCFA) for three months. I collapsed, and when I regained consciousness, I realized I was in the hospital. I could hardly think or make sense of all that was happening. All that came to mind were endless questions about human wickedness and greed. I realized the countless families Che had destroyed through his wickedness.

From 1981 to 1989, more than 20 sales boys were dismissed unjustly, receiving little or no compensation. Families that tried to contact the police were frustrated because Mr. Esi Okafor always used his money to win cases. The entire police force in the city seemed to be under his control. Those who received minimal compensation could hardly survive in business. Either their goods would sink into the sea, or a mysterious fire would burn down their shops, forcing them to close, leading to frustration. You could see them begging or helping in other shops to make a living. It was disguised slavery that needed God's intervention.

No one ever succeeded with money that came from Okafor. The strange practices he enforced in his shops and home, along with the evil words he directed at his workers, made us realize that he dedicated his riches to evil shrines. I was reminded of the Word of God that says, "The human heart is evil, and only God alone can understand and yield" (Jer. 17:5-10). Despite the frustration inflicted on families and sales boys by Okafor, no one dared to question what was going on. Our families seemed to have been blinded or brainwashed by the master's cunning practices. The little gifts they received from him made them content. All I knew was that things would never be the same, as my hopes and dreams had vanished. This phenomenon was common among Nigerian businesspeople against their salesboys, frustrating many Cameroonian families.

When Mr. Esi Okafor got the news of the stock shortage, he became furious. I can hardly describe the state of anger I witnessed. Tension, terror, and fear dominated the atmosphere, and he could hear nothing from anyone but how to get back his money. The first thing he did was close the shop where I was manager until further notice. A few days later, he handed me transport fare to return home and bring my parents and his money.

That night, before leaving for the village the next day, was the worst of my life. I experienced unbearable fear, shock, and nightmares filled with awful images and corpses attacking me in my dreams. The amount given for transport was exact; he gave me nothing extra to buy bread for my brothers and sisters, let alone my parents. It was an indication that the future was not going to be easy, and I wondered how my parents would take the news because it would be a great disappointment. That was eight years of wasted effort, and no one would easily believe I was innocent. I didn't know where to begin to clear myself in that situation. I was reminded of what the Bible says: "The love of money is the root of all evil and causes total ruin."

The next day at 4 a.m., there was a hard knock on our door by Mr. Okafor, shouting my name, "Christopher! … Christopher! … Get up; it is time for you to leave for the village. Go bring my money. That is all I need from you—rat and thief." I was so terrified that I missed my way to the door, and I hurried to get myself ready. I was so confused that I didn't have the strength to pray or think of anything.

Chapter VII - My Journey to the Village

By 5 a.m., I was already at the Ntarinkon Motor Park in Bamenda. It was May 1989. Nobody knew I was coming, as my parents had no means of communication. Mr. Okafor never bothered to inform them of my arrival. I knew deep down that such surprises could bring disaster. I wondered whether my brothers, sisters and some family members would recognize me. I was pale, having lost 10 kg in a few days. I had taken only a few clothes because he said I would barely have two or three days at home. Throughout the journey, my mind was busy, but I felt happy that I was going home to my people. I had not seen them for over seven years; it felt like a century. The thought comforted me greatly, as it was an opportunity to tell them what I had experienced all these years. I would recount every detail of Mr. Okafor and Che's evil machinations that had frustrated countless families.

I prayed to God to make them believe me. I hardly realized that five hours had passed, and we were already at Wum Park, where I was born and raised. The place was more degraded than it had been eight years ago. I wondered whether it was a curse on my people and our land. We believe so much in native doctors and evil practices; I concluded that such a people can hardly progress. I also looked strange to those who recognized me at the Motor Park. They were surprised I had returned home with only a small plastic bag after about eight years, as I had told them I did not have luggage. They did not believe me, and some thought I had sent my luggage home before arriving. I immediately trekked home, and I could barely recognize the village street. Our famous "Nyanga Street," where I grew up, and our compound looked dilapidated.

From the Wum Motor Park, news had reached my family that I was around due to the large crowd that was waiting. Some even trekked to the park to meet me, and those on the farm were rushing home to welcome me. They embraced me joyfully, and I sometimes found myself on the ground. I could hardly hold back my tears. I wept and wailed passionately, and soon the rest of them joined me as if we were bereaved. They were as amazed as the people at the Motor Park that I did not have any luggage; I had only a small plastic bag, like a primitive man. I could hardly recognize them. The parents I saw moved my heart with pity. All five of my mothers—my father's wives—along with my father, looked worn out from pressures and material poverty. All the same, they welcomed me as a true family would.

Food came from all the homes, and I ate to my satisfaction. They joined me in feasting, and my father brought out a ten-litre keg of palm wine. Our family discussion was scheduled for 5 p.m., and the rest of the day was meant for receiving visitors and learning more about the family and what my future would hold. Despite the abject poverty the family was enduring, they were happy and living in peace. I hardly experienced such happiness in the city, even among the richest. I confirmed that material riches, though necessary, do not bring true happiness, for my family found the real meaning of life. I wanted to be happy, but the constraint of being free from Mr. Okafor's greed and grip was a nightmare. I could barely answer the numerous questions from the crowd and my family members.

At 5 p.m., nobles from the Esu Royal Fondom and family members filled our parlour to hear my story. I began recounting my experiences from June 1981 to 1989 with Mr. Okafor. I spoke of slavery, horror, enslavement, evil practices, the brainwashing of workers and parents, and the frustration inflicted on countless families, then shared my true mission in the village. The whole assembly, including my father, was mourning; especially my mother. It was an unbearable sight. The family was disappointed with my former boss and his manager, and I was satisfied that they believed me. From 5 p.m. to 11 p.m., the atmosphere remained tense, and people were angry at my father. Some even accused him of selling me. Other nobles suggested that we consult the gods of the land, and they agreed.

Deciding to consult the gods was one thing; having the means to meet the demands and arrange for transportation was

Village life

another challenge. In our African tradition, you cannot approach the gods empty-handed. I wondered whether this was necessary and how it conformed to my Christian faith.

The more we planned for the journey to the gods, the more perplexed I became. It made me ask many questions, such as: Was it the will of God? I would have preferred to meet the pastor of the local

Presbyterian Church in Naikom-Overside. As a prince from a royal lineage, consulting the gods was automatic in such situations, so there was no way I could influence their decisions. It took us three days to be ready to embark on this journey, and although my siblings were generous enough to share some of their clothing with me, I still looked tattered. Thank God we arrived safely in Esu.

It was a great relief for me to be in my home village and among my people. Despite the mediocre level of development and poverty, I noticed that they lived in love and were convivial. Seeing how happy they were and how they survived on their peasant farming, I wondered how they could express so much love and happiness while the rich, who had everything, lacked true love and happiness. For the first time in my life, I was amazed by the hospitality with which they received us. Food came from every kitchen in the palace to welcome us, while the notables brought palm wine. Our small meal turned into a welcome party when I tasted the sweetest palm wine. I felt like the Prodigal Son. All those present to welcome us showered me with love, and I felt nostalgic.

Later that evening, there was a gathering of the notables to discuss the reason for our visit. I narrated everything I had gone through—the pain, torture, enslavement, and accusations levied against me. The more I spoke, the more I could see anger and pain on their faces, but they remained calm and listened to me until the end. After hearing everything I said, the notables were bitter and made my struggles their problem. They rebuked my father for pushing me into such a situation. To them, it felt like he had sold me, from royal blood to such cruel people. They warned my father and instructed him never to do such a thing again. They also advised other parents not to listen only to their tutors but also to their children when handing them over to their tutors—something my father never did. He kept rebuking me each time I complained, thinking the man had a plan for me. He was made to vow never to send any other child to such a place. The villagers also swore that no person of royal blood would become a slave and that it should be a lesson to all villagers to be more careful and wiser in their dealings, ensuring that they reach concrete agreements.

They carried out the necessary procedures to consult the gods, and the revelations made were significant. They revealed that Che was a manipulator who used his talents to embezzle Mr. Esi Okafor's wealth. Che exploited Mr. Okafor's illiteracy to enrich himself, and he did not stop there. He also used his position to frustrate the salesboys who profited under his master, like the Bad Steward in the Holy Scriptures who embezzled the wealth of his master (Luke 16:1-13). Mr. Okafor belonged to a secret society or cult that specialized in exploiting children, frustrating them to their content. I was overwhelmed yet relieved, as the findings vindicated me and proved that everything I had once spoken of or complained about was true. I worshipped God for setting me free from bondage.

In the end, they decided that a delegation would accompany me to Bamenda to declare my innocence and reveal all the findings. My people took it as a war, one in which they fought to vindicate their son and all the children who suffered in Mr. Okafor's hands. They agreed to give him a final ultimatum: either he confirmed my innocence, or something would happen. The way my people handled the problem and their determination to see it through to the end made me feel fulfilled, but deep down, I wished never to go there again. Unfortunately, there was no way I could escape it.

Chapter VIII - My Return to Bamenda

Arrangements to leave for Bamenda were not easy due to financial constraints. The royal family had to sell off some goats and fowl to raise money for a delegation of six, including me: three notables, my dad, and my uncle. My uncle, a prison warden, opted to pay his own transportation fare. The entire family was downcast and disappointed at such misfortune befalling their son. My mother and younger siblings never stopped weeping. Some said, "We hoped he would become the family breadwinner, but it is all in vain. When will good things ever come to us? Others go and succeed, but it is always different for us!" Some attributed it to curses, while others referred to the anger of the gods. For me, gods or no gods, curses or no curses, ancestral or not, nothing is above God. I was more interested in seeing how the problem would be resolved, and I believed that the prayers I was making would vindicate my family and me.

In November 1989, we set out for Bamenda. Upon our arrival at the shop on Commercial Avenue around 10 a.m., we were immediately taken to Mr. Okafor's residence on Savana Street, Mankon. Those who accompanied us were given strict instructions to keep us in an isolated area until he returned. Thank God they provided us with something to eat and drink from a nearby restaurant. At about 4 p.m., he arrived with several Nigerian businessmen, including the manager. The atmosphere was tense, and fear coursed through me, confirming that it was not going to be easy. With the living room arranged for the meeting, I quickly rushed into our room to change, as I had brought only a few clothes when I left for the village. To my dismay, I found my bag torn open, with all my dresses in pieces, smeared with oil and strange powder. Confused, I carried the bag to the meeting place in tears, and they thought I was mad. Mr. Esi Okafor immediately addressed the meeting, saying, "We have gathered to know whether you have brought my money. If not, we are wasting a lot of time. I will take drastic action. I trusted you, but you want to kill me."

Mr. Okafor took time to explain to those present at the meeting everything that had happened—how he trusted me and the promise he made to my father to make me the best. All of this effort was made without knowing I was stabbing him in the back. The manager added that I was among the best, but he did not understand how I had squandered so much money. Had he not intervened, it would have been worse. They did their best to taint my reputation and portray me as the villain. Some Nigerian businessmen commented that no salesboy should be trusted because they always mismanage their masters' businesses while still expecting to be compensated. "The one you trust among these boys will be the one to stab you in the end," they remarked. Others shared glaring examples of boys who had bankrupted them. Some advised me and my parents to do everything possible to resolve the issue, or else it would not be easy. They also praised my master for being such a good person by helping Cameroonians and other boys escape misery, while we, on the other side, took it for granted. When they finished, they gave us the floor.

I was the first to speak. I explained how I started working in the company and how they conducted the audit without involving us. We only saw the results on the manager's table. From 1981 to 1989, none of my stock audits had ever failed, yet in just three months, he claimed I had a shortage. God knows I am not guilty, and I suspected there was a conspiracy to destabilize my position in the company because they did not give me the chance to participate in the audits.

I opened my bag and poured out all my belongings that I had left behind before going to the village. They were all torn into pieces and mixed with strange substances. I could not hold back the tears streaming down my cheeks. I told them, "I am ready to undergo anything, but you should know that God will vindicate me from this conspiracy. If we are talking about stabbing, you are the ones stabbing me because my stocks have never had any problems for the past eight years, so why now?" I also pointed out that during my time there, twenty boys had been sent away for theft or womanizing with little or no compensation. If my master and the manager were serious about helping me, why had I never participated in the stock audit?

"Please, name any of your sales boys who have ever succeeded in your company." Additionally, he never agreed to sign a contract with my family concerning my stay.

At this juncture, he angrily stared at me and got up to hit me, using words like "thief, I will show you, you will go to prison." Had the crowd not stopped him, I would have landed on the floor. My uncle, the prison warden, warned him sternly to stop making noise because they were not there to joke. He called Mr. Okafor an ungrateful man and said he should not frighten us with empty threats because the law would take its course. The fact that there was no agreement between him and the rest of the servants meant he would face the consequences for exploiting innocent children and families, thereby destabilizing their futures and aspirations. "Don't think we do not know what you Nigerians are doing to our people in this country. The time has come for it to stop. It is too much. Who do you think you are? So, you think only salesboys steal while masters are angels? Look at how agitated our son is!" Mr Okafor was breathing heavily and sweating like someone who had just run a horse race. I thought he would faint. Then my uncle concluded, "We have come to hold you responsible for all this misfortune. The nobles will tell us the results of their findings."

The king's spokesman took over. He began by saying that the king had sent them to greet Mr Okafor and to help him correct himself and the manager for their evil concoction against innocent families. "For your information, Christopher comes from a noble family; he is a prince, and no noble can be mistreated and go free. The king sent us to consult the ancestors. The voice of the gods of the land made it clear that your manager does not want anyone to take the upper hand in your business. He has put a spell on you so that whatever he tells you, you take it as gospel truth."

At this point, the manager got mad. I had never seen a wild beast like him almost attacking the family with his hands, and my father was in tears. Even those present were shaking their heads in amazement. The other Nigerian businessmen called for calm and pleaded that everyone be allowed to speak until the end. They began speaking in their dialect. One notable added:

"Your manager here has businesses and houses all over the place that you do not know about. He deals with native doctors and does not want anyone to take his place. Our gods do not lie. As an important person in your village, you can make inquiries, and they will tell you because you are also involved in many evil practices. Several times, you brought many evil spells from your country to hang in your shops and have your boys cross over them, swearing never to steal from you, or else they get mad. According to you, who can be a salesboy and not even pick something? Are you not a thief yourself for exploiting people?"

Another notable added, "If they reject the evidence, the consequences will not be drastic. Our son has brought his bag of clothes torn into pieces, and no one has talked about it. All you are concerned about is your money." They examined the clothes and were dumbfounded. The delegation called ten boys to the scene and questioned them about this evil act, but to no avail. Fear was evident on their faces as they crowded in one corner. It proved how traumatizing working for Mr. Okafor was. The notable concluded, "The ball is in your court, and you will have to settle our son, whom you enslaved for over eight years, depriving him of many things, even the opportunity to come and visit the ancestors. Do you think you can waste him like that? Never!"

Esi Okafor had five children: four boys and a girl—Okamaka, Nnamdi, Ifeanyi, Azuka, and Chinedu. They were all educated in Cameroon and continued to Nigeria after writing JAMB. After they completed their studies, they did their youth service. Most of them were medical students and pharmacists. They all approved of my working skills, and we got along easily.

Nigerians in the Diaspora rarely keep their children outside the country, especially their daughters, either for fear of them marrying foreigners or getting pregnant before marriage. They hardly marry foreigners, no matter the circumstances. We were always disappointed with Cameroonian girls who pursued these Nigerian men and had children with them, only for the Nigerians to later abandon them. My shock was how Esi Okafor's children turned against me when they heard of the stock shortage. I realized that no one should entrust themselves to another human being (Ps 118, Sirach 6: 6-17). I am sure they participated in destroying my belongings at home, which I considered vanity of vanities. I, therefore, concluded that being attached to the things of this world makes you an enemy of God (James 4: 1-10, 1 John 2: 15-17).

Chapter IX - The Way Forward

A spell seemed to have fallen off Mr Esi Okafor's mind as he called for a private consultation with the Nigerian businessmen present. After about ten minutes, he returned, and everything took another turn. The differences were now between Mr. Okafor and the manager. After thanking the notables and those who had come, he recounted how the manager had been against all who worked for him and had created problems throughout the years. He advised against having contracts with families and always made up stories. He had orchestrated the dismissal of these sales boys with little or no settlement against his wishes. He went on to recount all the times he had questioned the manager about the chequebooks signed without his authorization and the business transactions made without any feedback. The more he spoke, the more you could feel the anger rising within him. He lamented how the manager had taken advantage of his illiteracy to enrich himself. He declared he would not let the matter rest but would take it to court for justice to prevail.

The manager tried to defend himself to no avail. The more he attempted to counter Mr. Okafor's points, the higher the tension rose. It escalated to the point that the Nigerian businessmen had to intervene, speaking bitterly to the manager while interrogating him. "Is what your master is saying true? Have you withdrawn money without his authorization? Have you conducted transactions without his knowledge? Are you ready to swear to the gods? Because if we take this to our kinsmen, you will regret it."

Then Mr. Okafor added, "Even if you have shares in the business, you have no right to carry out any transaction without my knowledge. I trusted you, yet you bewitched me!" He ended up weeping like a child, and it was difficult to console him. I was amazed at what was happening; a disagreement between them had never occurred throughout my time with them. The notables commented in the dialect amid the tension that our gods had spoken and the eyes of my master had opened. Though he was also a wicked man, no wicked person wants wickedness meted out to him. I praised God Almighty for His marvels and for vindicating me. It made me remember the Holy Scriptures, which say, "Don't worry about what you will say, for I will give you an eloquence that no one will be able to challenge" (Lk 21:5-19).

Esi Okafor signed a cheque for four hundred thousand francs and handed it to my father at about 8 p.m. He said, "This will enable Christopher to manage until we sort out the case." My uncle seized the cheque and threw it back at him.

"Do you think we are fools? What is FCFA 400,000 for eight years of slavery?" The eldest Nigerian businessman intervened, saying, "This is not the final settlement. It will enable Christopher to manage until the investigation is over. We will hire a chartered accountant and a lawyer to investigate, audit, and control the stock and punish the crook." But my uncle insisted on knowing if such an amount could settle a servant who had served for eight years. This led to a new bargain as if they had just started the service. In the end, Mr. Esi Okafor said, "If all is well, I will write a cheque for two million as a settlement," Mr. Esi concluded.

After consultations with the families and notables, they decided that the freedom of their son was far greater than all the money in the world. "If it were not for our gods, our son would have long been killed, as most of such people are fond of rituals." They blamed the family for not concluding matters from the beginning and vowed never to give any sons or daughters of the soil into such slavery. The notables then addressed the assembly, saying, "We are taking back the message to our king and will be leaving with our son tonight until your investigations are over, but he will be in town to think of what to do while waiting." Mr. Esi Okafor confirmed that I had to be around because they needed my statement during the investigation.

That night, at about 9 p.m., we left for Brassaries Street, Mankon, Bamenda, to my brother Chi Albert's house. Thank God the Nigerian businessmen offered the delegation FCFA 100,000 for transport. Some Nigerian businessmen said I should come and see them, and Mr.

Okafor added that it would not be long before they would need me. He collected my brother's contact details to reach me if and when necessary. When leaving, I abandoned all my clothes and shoes to start a new life.

They received us at about 9:45 p.m. The Esu elite was waiting for our arrival. They set a table with a variety of food and were eager to hear us recount our journey. While the notables narrated the story, I was still in disbelief about my freedom, and my uncle swore to deal with Mr Okafor if nothing good came out of this because it was not yet over. "He cannot use our son as a slave and go scot-free," he said. All the notables responded, "Amen" in the dialect.

I considered the feasting a freedom party for me, and it was also a welcome party for my brother, Chi Albert, who had just moved to Bamenda from Kumba. During the feast, there was a brief meeting in which the notables advised me on how to face life in the future. They emphasized my origin, which is meant to guide me in living my life, for no royalty is found living a wayward life, and I should avoid being carried away by city life, which has enticed many to their downfall. My brother's transfer to Bamenda was a blessing, as he happened to be there at the right time. The notables gave him the authority to watch over me and to follow Mr Okafor and his manager's activities regarding the investigation, constantly updating them on the evolution of events.

They concluded with special ancestral blessings, asking that the ancestors keep their son in peace and give him the wisdom to manage every step of his life, to be helpful to the world, and that no enemy should ever conquer him. They spoke over palm wine to the gods to accept these blessing rites, pouring some in front of the door and around me. The notables drank from the libation cup before offering it to me as well. They concluded the blessing rites by each putting spittle on my head. I recalled the powerful blessings given to me by my grandfather in 1980. It was a fun-filled evening, and I felt ready to face the future. I pity those who refuse to live according to their culture and traditions, especially the youth who do so under the banner of modernism. After enjoying the festivities and a little rest, the notables departed for the village at 5 a.m. from the Ntarinkon Motor Park.

After the settlement

Chapter X - Life After Esi Okafor

After the departure of the notables, I took some time to rest and reflect. I decided to present my ancestral blessings to God, the greatest Ancestor, in case any idol worship was involved. For the first time, I experienced the best sleep ever. It was comforting, especially considering how wonderful life in the family was. The unity, love, sharing, togetherness, and advice I received made it all the more special and helped me become more conscious of myself. Consequently, I regained my sense of identity. The healing process was rapid, and things seemed to move faster. I got myself new clothes, which felt strange to me. For the first time, I bought things for myself. I also helped my brother organize his hawking business, and he travelled from one village to another selling his products. He mostly visited neighbouring villages like Batibo, Mbengwi, Bali, and Bafut.

Mr. Okafor called my brother after two to meet him and start the investigation, as the case was already in court. He took me to Lawyer Sendze's Chambers in Ntamulung Quarter to give my statement, which I did. The lawyer asked questions, and I answered them. They drilled me several times to prepare me to appear in court as Okafor's witness.

My brother advised me to start something to occupy my time while waiting for the court case to be resolved, as it would take some time. An opportunity immediately arose on Ringway Street in Bamenda, where I found a small shop close to my former workplace. My brother invested in the business by paying six months' rent and fixing counters. I used the FCFA 400,000 given to me to meet various businesspeople who supplied goods to stock the shop while I repaid the balance from my sales. That was a clear result of God's divine intervention and the ancestral blessings I received. I started with goods worth FCFA 2.5

million, including electrical and building materials. Since my brother was Catholic and I was Presbyterian, he advised me to bring a priest to bless the place. That was in 1992. Rev. Fr. Atang advised me to conduct my business with God always in mind because, these days, Satan has taken over many businesses. Whether you like it or not, they will all return to Satan because he always takes whatever he gives. That was a fresh reminder, and I quickly recognized what he meant.

It was a good start because all my customers seemed to have returned, while my former shop remained closed. When I was informed of the first court hearing, I could not sleep. When the day finally came, I was surprised by the number of people who came to hear the case. It was a celebrity case that shook the Bamenda business community. They called me to testify against Mr. Okafor's manager. The court attendant summoned me to the bar and taught me how to swear on the Bible. I was instructed to say, "I swear to tell the truth and nothing but the truth."

Lawyer Sendze began by asking me questions, and when he finished, the manager's lawyer pounced on me, accusing me of all sorts of things and calling me a thief and a liar. He attributed the entire case to me and concluded by accusing me of being bribed by Mr Okafor to lie against his client, thereby transferring the responsibility for my alleged crimes to an innocent man. Okafor was so angry and agitated that he became uncivil towards the lawyer, prompting the judge to call him to order.

The lawyer continued, stating that the shortage discovered was from my stock, so why was I accusing his client? Mr. Okafor's lawyer called him to order, and the judge cautioned him to ask questions and not lay accusations. That day, the chartered accountant audited and reported being shocked to discover haphazard business transactions conducted over the years. This revelation made Okafor even more agitated. He exclaimed, "You see, I told you that the man was a thief, a killer, and you are here accusing me of bribery. You will return my money, or else you will go to prison." The judge again called him to order. The manager and his witnesses denied some of the accusations levelled against him, doing all they could to defend themselves.

It was a very long hearing that day, and the court adjourned the case

for three months. After the hearing,

Babysitting the Fouda children

my family decided I should find a place to live while managing my business. That month, I found a place at the end of Tar Longla Street and furnished it with a modern studio. Most of the contractors who came to my former shop became my regular customers, and in two to three months, I had made a profit of about FCFA 500,000. I was advised to open an account at the Ntarikon Credit Union to support my business.

The court adjourned the case several times, and by July 1993, I had virtually paid off 80 per cent of my debt and was planning to take a loan from the Ntarikon Credit Union in December. However, before that could happen, my relationship with Mr. Okafor became stressful. He started behaving strangely towards me. As soon as he noticed that most of his customers were patronizing me, and people told him I was doing well, he developed this odd behaviour. I pretended not to notice these changes, and when he passed by my street, he didn't even look in the direction of my shop or reply when I greeted him.

In October 1993, the case ended. Esi Okafor recovered most of his wealth from what the manager had stolen, and they parted ways with an amicable settlement. In November, nightmares became the order of the day. I could not get a good night's sleep. As soon as I went to bed and closed my eyes, Okafor would appear on a screen, warning me about taking all his customers and accusing me of avoiding taking goods from him while sourcing from other businesspeople. He claimed that I had declared war on him, which would take my life if I didn't close my shop. I had hoped he would give me my complete settlement after the case, but that did not happen. As days went by, the situation worsened. I would open the shop, then abandon it to stroll around town, leaving it unattended until evening. Customers would come, but I couldn't attend to them until I returned to close the shop.

This situation persisted for a while, and many people began to wonder what was wrong with me. The dreams were recurrent, but eventually, they changed. The more Mr. Okafor appeared to warn me, the more the Blessed Virgin Mary appeared as the Immaculate Conception to save me, presenting thousands of suffering children and youths. I reported this to Pastor Perfock at the Presbyterian Church in Ntamulung. They attributed her appearance to an evil mermaid and began praying to cast her away, but the more they prayed, the more she appeared. News spread to the village that I was mad, and my brother said he could not understand what was happening to me and needed quick intervention. The reply he received was that Mr Esi Okafor was dealing with money dedicated to the gods of a shrine and wanted to sacrifice me for rituals. He suggested that I should abandon everything in the shop and run away.

The dreams continued, and the scenario remained the same. Okafor kept threatening me, while Our Lady protected me and revealed many other things. This situation prompted me to meet with a Catholic priest, as advised by the family of Ndi Nyah Regina, my shop neighbour who had adopted me as their son. She was a devoted Christian at St. Theresia Parish in Small Mankon. I confided in her, and she took me to meet the parish priest, Rev. Fr. Michael Kintang. After presenting my case to him, he told me that Our Lady wanted me to serve her and advised me to ask her what my mission was as soon as I got home. I explained that I was a Presbyterian and had not been taught how to serve Mary but rather Christ. I have never seen an angry priest in my life. He became furious and said,

"My friend, Protestant, what are your Protestants still protesting against? What do you even know about Christianity? Are the 99 points not enough? How dare you challenge the Mother of God and humanity? Leave my office and wait for her to tell you what to do."

In the end, he sprinkled holy water on me, made the sign of the cross on my forehead, and asked me to report any incidents that occurred. That night, only Mary appeared in my dreams; Mr. Okafor was nowhere to be found. She showed me crowds of reckless infants, children, and young people, then left without saying anything. When I woke up that night, I was sweating profusely, as if it had rained on me. I longed to return to the priest, but the night felt endless. Early the next morning, I told him what had happened, and he replied that it was what Our Lady wanted from me. He explained that the reckless crowds I had seen signified the lost souls I needed to fight to bring back to the Lord, and that she would accompany me on this mission. The message was so clear that I did not hesitate to tell him I wanted to become a Catholic. He wrote a note, which I took to the catechist for direct enrollment in doctrine classes. The catechist instructed that I should have extra classes to catch up with the other catechumens.

During my time of insanity, my family asked my younger brother, Jude Kawzu, to come and assist me while he was schooling at GHS Bamenda. When I told him the news that I was becoming Catholic, he was surprised and exclaimed, "How come! What will the pastors and Christians say?" That Sunday, when they did not see me in church, my brother informed them of my decision the following week. Some elders and youths came to my house, calling it treason and betrayal. They wondered why I had left when the whole church was praying for me. They asked me to come and see the pastor. I had made up my mind, and it was so strong that no one could easily take it from me.

I wanted nothing else but to follow my vocation, and the one question I asked them was, "Why do we say in our credo, born of the Virgin, and I believe in the Holy Catholic Church?" Yet they could not give me any concrete response. A veil seemed to have lifted from me when I started the doctrine classes. I thought of Saul, a great persecutor of believers, who was captured by the Lord on his way to Damascus (Acts of the Apostles, chapter 9). I realized that I had persecuted many innocent people and the Church of Christ, and I regretted it profoundly. I was ready to make amends, as St. Paul did. The priest's words had a powerful effect on me, similar to what Ananias did for Saul because from that day, the nightmares and the appearances of the Blessed Virgin Mary ceased.

Despite my zeal to continue on my newfound path, my Presbyterian brothers and sisters kept disturbing me, saying I was possessed and wondering how I could abandon the God of Scriptures for the so-called Blessed Virgin Mary. To them, Mary is just a used envelope that does not have a place in the salvation of souls. It made me wonder how I would feel if my mother, who gave birth to and raised me, was called a used envelope, especially now that I am grown up and crowned with many achievements.

The new doctrine classes were interesting, and I caught up quickly, asking all the questions that made me doubt the Catholic faith. I learned that Jesus Christ founded the Catholic Church (Matthew 16: 13-20) and handed the authority to Peter, who became the first pope and Christ's representative on earth. I also learned that "catholic" means universal and is hierarchically linked to the Pope. Additionally, I discovered that the Protestant Bible contains 66 books, while the Catholic Bible has 73 because some Protestants and Pentecostals removed certain chapters and verses that did not suit them.

I was taught that Martin Luther was an Augustinian priest who decided to quit due to the sale of indulgences and sacraments. I learned that there are only two sacraments (baptism and marriage) in the Protestant Church, whereas the Catholic Church recognizes seven: baptism, confirmation, communion, penance, anointing of the sick, marriage, and holy orders, which are all essential for salvation. I was amazed by the richness of the doctrine and how well the catechist mastered it. From time to time, a priest would come and teach us about the Bible and some dogmas. I realized that I had been living in gross ignorance and was ready to return to my brothers to clarify what was happening concerning Christianity.

It was a scandal for me to learn that people could reject the Bible compiled by Christ's Church. Without the Catholic Church, the Bible would never have existed, and all holy places would remain unsecuritized. Catholics own ninety per cent of all holy places in the world. Mary also plays a role in salvation through her apparitions and the Rosary, a summary of the New Testament and the lives of Jesus and Mary—something I had hated with all my heart without understanding. I concluded that ignorance is damnation.

I had decided to abandon the shop as soon as I took the sacraments because each time I went there, my life was never the same. Living through the Lenten season from February 1994 to Holy Saturday night was transformative. I experienced an inner change and realized that the Catholic Church does not make noise but lives its faith. It was on April 2, 1994, that I was admitted to the Catholic Church, confirmed, and received the Holy Eucharist, the body of Christ. I began living my Catholic faith by attending Mass every day to break the spell that haunted me, asking God to show me the way through the Blessed Virgin Mary. My elder brother, Chi Albert, was the only one who was happy about my newfound faith, while my mom was reticent and vowed never to step foot in the Catholic Church. I smiled at this and prayed that time would enlighten my mother.

Until then, Mr. Esi Okafor had not called to settle my debts, and I was ready to give up everything, even the shop, to find peace. It was needless to carry on with a business built on impure money, which would end in disaster like that of many young people who served such masters. Mr. Okafor's situation was even worse; he was critically ill and looked pale. I dropped Mr. Okafor a note, asking him to take everything I had in my shop and to understand that he had not settled me to date. I informed all my family members not to direct him to where I was, yet he kept bothering my brother about my whereabouts. Before dropping him the note, I had borrowed FCFA two hundred thousand, which I invested in procuring travel bags for sale to start a new life in Yaoundé. I also informed the landlord about Mr Okafor coming to empty the shop and left him with the keys. I did my best not to start my new life with anything directly or indirectly related to my former boss.

In June 1994, I received blessings from the parish priest, Fr. Kintang Michael, and then left for Yaoundé after also receiving blessings from my family. My younger brother, Kum Jude Kwazu, was to join my elder brother at Brasseries Street in Bamenda, as he was to write the GCE Ordinary Level. Throughout the journey, I was restless, haunted by nightmares as I wondered how my new life would be in my uncle and contractor, Pa Ben Chu Ewoh's house. The only thing I was sure of was that I would not compromise my faith for anything. My cousins and nephews received me warmly at Mokolo Elobi, Yaoundé, because my uncle had already retired to the village.

Chapter XI - Life In Yaoundé

I must say, Mokolo Elobi was an environment I never knew existed in this world. Since arriving, I had never seen such a harsh setting, and this was where I would spend my new life. At the time, Mokolo Elobi was one of the messiest areas in Cameroon, situated in a swampy environment that resembled a Hysacam deposit zone. We dreaded the rainy season so much that we prayed for a dry season throughout the year. Each time it rained, the whole place turned into a pool, filled with all sorts of things floating—kitchen utensils, household items, waste from the gutters, and even faeces from emptied toilets.

The infrastructure in the quarter didn't help; everywhere was dotted with dilapidated "carabot" houses that seemed to welcome the floods each time it rained. During the rainy season, there was little difference between someone living on the streets and us. It was just the tip of the iceberg, as even the living conditions in this area were subpar. The inhabitants looked frail and malnourished; each time I saw them, I immediately thought of patients suffering from terminal diseases. Mosquitoes didn't make things any easier, nearly draining them of the blood left in their systems, which made them look weaker and sicker, with malaria being a constant threat.

I was downcast and imagined how my uncle and his children were so proud to be residents of Yaoundé. How could a big contractor, who had built mansions for many in the city, live in such an environment yet be unable to construct a decent house for himself, even in the village? I could not comprehend how Yaoundé, the capital city of Cameroon, could have such a neighbourhood. "This surely means that the country is cursed," I thought. I almost considered leaving the city for somewhere else, but one of my cousins encouraged me to promote my business and pursue other opportunities there. He said, "Your life will not end here. Just persevere and work hard; once you make money, you can relocate to a better place. I assure you, there are beautiful places here in Yaoundé, but if you want to live there, you must make money." He urged me not to worry, adding that it is a town for all walks of life and that anyone can succeed simply by visiting the right places. What he said made sense. If I had to change, where would I get the money? As the saying goes, "A beggar has no choice."

My cousins began to initiate me into the business, taking me around to show me the main streets of Yaoundé. They advised me to sell my bags by hawking around the town, as this method would provide a quicker and higher turnover compared to having a defined sales point. I agreed as they emphasized that having a sales point was riskier because council workers could seize my goods at any time. I began hawking, but my worst handicap was the French language. The business was slow; I could barely sell a bag a day, and it was from this that I had to feed myself, especially since moving around town was stressful and tiring. I used to hawk from Mokolo Elobi to Central Town, Mvog-Ada, Essos, Mimboman, Omnisport, Ngoussou, Etoudi, Nlongkak, Ecole de Police, and finally back home.

During the first two weeks, I developed many blisters and experienced so much tiredness that I had to take some time off from the business. I located a small wall where I could hang the bags for display. Sometimes, I auctioned some of the bags to have money to buy food and take care of myself. The market was so rough that I thought I was cursed. One thing my cousin did not warn me about was the presence of bandits and pickpockets. But it wasn't long before I learned about them the hard way. I discovered this truth when thieves stole some of my goods and shoes at the Central Post. The items they robbed me of stayed on my mind. It may sound funny, but I lived in a bandit-infested area, especially since there was a gang of armed robbers led by one Billy, who spent most of their time burglarizing and attacking with all sorts of weapons. Many times, police officers and gendarmes would come and arrest him and some of his gang members, but you would still see them moving about freely the following day as if nothing had happened.

Despite these happenings, I still had to learn this bitter truth the hard way. Sometimes, you never know when and how a robbery takes place; you only realize it when you start searching for your stolen items. I was shocked to learn that gangsters are at the centre of this line of work! It was one of the many issues I had to cope with, especially the constant police and gendarme raids known as calé, which only worsened matters. Each time they came through our quarter, we found ourselves giving explanations at the police station under severe pressure not to disclose or even mention Billy's name for fear of the consequences we might face when we returned home, as he had threatened us never to. One might think we looked like hoodlums or gang members living nearby, but it was just a common occurrence that anyone could find themselves as a result of being in the wrong place at the wrong time. In my case, you can guess what the wrong place was. Living in Elobi surpassed even the wrong time because 24/7 was the wrong time.

After some hardships and perseverance, I began to think of another line of business. Just then, my elder brother, Bong Simon, from the Southwest Region of Cameroon, started coming to Yaoundé to supply goods. He dealt with cosmetics and suggested I join him if my business was not going well by helping to deliver cosmetics wholesale to retailers. I agreed and was entitled to a commission on the profit, which helped me survive. My younger brother, Akap Augustine, later joined us from the Southwest to engage in hawking, but they only spent a few days with us because they had to go get more goods each time they finished sales. Being around my family members comforted me, though the battle remained tough.

As far as my spiritual life was concerned, I attended Sunday Masses at St. Joseph Catholic Church in Elig-Efa. On the third Sunday in that community, I was approached by some young people, Brothers Paul Egbwe and Fidelis Abang, who said, "The Blessed Virgin Mary has spoken to us to invite you to join the Legion of Mary." It was another nightmare for me. I retorted, "Where did the Blessed Virgin Mary see me to send you to take me to the Legion of Mary? *Abeg, una leave me ya;* I am a Presbyterian. I am not a full Catholic yet, and you are asking me to join your group. *Wety be Legion of Mary sef?*" Their patience and humility amazed me. Despite my response, they still pleaded with me to give them some time to explain what the Legion of Mary was all about.

As they spoke, my memory quickly rushed back to Bamenda, where I remembered my encounter with the Blessed Virgin Mary and how she showed me miserable children at the seashore. The more they spoke, the more my heartbeat accelerated. I listened attentively. If I remember correctly, they said the Legion of Mary was founded by a lay faithful, Frank Duff, in Ireland, inspired by the Holy Spirit to live the spirituality and virtues of the Blessed Virgin Mary to crush the head of the serpent and win souls for Christ. They described the group as a spiritual army whose weapons are prayer, especially the rosary, and holiness *(Legion Handbook, pages 9-13)*.

That night, it was clear that the Blessed Virgin Mary was watching over me, holding my hands, and taking care of me, so I needed to be careful. It completely changed my perspective on life, and I confirmed that God uses His saints to look after His people on earth, especially the mother of our Savior. However, when I thought of the way people lived in this world—power mongers, wickedness of all sorts, hatred and jealousy, and a love for money, especially Mr Esi Okafor and his manager, who treated many innocent people most cruelly and selfishly—I wondered whether people were attentive to the ways of God. It was clear that she was inviting me to join her army to fight the enemy of Christ in the world, and there was no way for me to resist. I knew the first battle zone would be my household, as my family members never cared about the things of God. They were all about money, never keeping the Sabbath day holy, and their way of life was far from ideal. This disturbed me the most, for anything can happen when you live with people who neither fear God nor pray.

The Legion of Mary received me the following Sunday with a warm welcome. I had found a true family of loving people who cared deeply about the things of God. It felt like a real family, for no matter your social rank or status, we addressed each other as brother and sister—we were all siblings in Christ. The group was well organized, and people spoke in turns, reporting on their activities. It was reminiscent of the mission of the twelve disciples in the Bible (Matthew 10:1-12) when they were sent out two by two and returned to give their reports to Christ. The president, Brother Fidelis Abang, introduced me and expressed his joy at having me with them. When he finished, it was my turn to introduce myself.

When I told them my name, my journey, my encounter with the Blessed

Virgin Mary, and my precarious condition, I saw tears dripping from the cheeks of some members. They were thrilled to see a former Presbyterian among them. They hugged me and assured me that I was in the right place—Mary's home—where she had wanted me to come long ago, so I should feel at home. They gave me a Legion Handbook and some prayer materials, saying, "The soldier is always with his armour." They advised me to pray without ceasing because the devil would always be an obstacle to our accomplishments in this world. I was so happy that I returned home determined to dedicate my life to serving God in the Legion of Mary. It was the most joyful day since I arrived in Yaoundé. From that day on, things were never the same again.

I began facing many challenges with a new spirit, accepting tough times with happiness and determination. Life in the swamps was not easy. In August and September, life became unbearable due to frequent floods that destroyed almost everything we had. Sometimes, at 3 a.m., we battled the floods until early morning. Additionally, I had to navigate between my business and my Legionary work. It was a very tedious and tiring time filled with many trials. But I found Our Lady encouraging and guiding me through these challenges. Though I had no clue where I was heading or what my future held, I kept going with the hope of seeing the sun again. Sometimes, legionary duties took us to Elig-Edjoa and other quarters in Yaoundé to preach the Word of God, and we often returned very late at night.

We formed Small Christian Communities and encouraged many families to receive Church sacraments. We also followed up on our activities. The acting president, Abang Fidelis, had to leave for the seminary in October, and all the members of Our Lady Queen of Peace Presidium unanimously nominated me as the acting president. I took over the animation of the Cadets of Mary with Mami Ancella Fanso and Madam Ekolle Stella. We began spreading both groups to all the parishes in Yaoundé, Mbalmayo, and Ebolowa. It was a fulfilment of what the Blessed Virgin Mary had shown me in my vision. Like St. Paul, I did it with zeal and determination. It shaped my prayer life and my way of thinking and living, pushing me to reconnect with one of my business friends in Bamenda, Mr. Ndefru Linus, popularly known as Betterman.

Chapter XII - My New Life

Mr. Linus Ndehfru, alias Betterman, was a struggling young businessman I met in Bamenda while working with Mr. Okafor. Like me, he comes from a royal background, being an offspring of the Mankon Palace. He moved to Yaoundé after his baptism in the Presbyterian Church in Ntamalung, Bamenda, in 1995. His goal was to expand his business by searching for new ways to buy and supply seasonal goods to other businesspeople.

One day, while I was at my usual spot where I hung my bags in Mokolo, I heard someone call my name, *"Christopher, weti you di do for here?"* As I turned, I saw a tall, fresh-looking young man whom I immediately recognized as Betterman, my friend from long ago. We fell into each other's arms and hugged so tightly that those around us watched in wonder. Some murmured to each other, trying to figure out our relationship. While some speculated that he was a relative or a friend, one exclaimed, *"C'est sûrement son ami qui n'est pas au pays. Sa vie va sûrement changer hein."*

He immediately took me to a nearby snack bar, leaving the speculators to their speculations. As we sat there, we recounted our past and what had been going on in our lives since we lost contact. I narrated everything I had been through, and we both wept over the difficulties and turmoil we had faced. We barely touched the food and drinks we ordered due to the overwhelming emotions.

That same day, he asked to see where I was living, so I parked my things and led the way. Thank God it didn't rain that day. As he stepped into the area, he could barely keep up with me. His well-polished shoes got muddy, and he had to jump or go around certain paths to avoid further dirtying himself. He struggled to keep up until he reached the house, visibly uncomfortable.

He didn't even sit down before exclaiming, "You know what? I'm going to take you out of this place. You are leaving this place now!" He was so disgusted and couldn't understand how I had ended up there. Taking a deep breath, he exclaimed, "What a world!" He then inquired, "So you mean your master gave you four hundred thousand francs after all the years you spent with him? What a wicked world!"

"Yes, brother," I answered. "I already told you everything," I explained that it wouldn't be possible to leave at that time, as I needed to discuss it with my family and explain that my stay with them had ended. He understood.

As I went to see him off, we stood for hours talking. During our discussion, he mentioned that he almost didn't recognize me because I had grown so pale. I laughed and said, "Na life," and we continued talking. We would have loved to go on, but we had to stop due to his business appointment. He gave me his business card so I could contact him as soon as I had discussed things with my family for him to pick me up. He also handed me FCFA twenty thousand, an amount I hadn't seen or touched for a long time.

That day, I couldn't comprehend my emotions. Heaven had surely intervened in my life. I wanted to exclaim with joy, but I also wanted to cry; I didn't know which to choose. One thing was clear: my life was about to change, and I felt something significant was about to happen. I wondered what my new life would be like outside Mokolo Elobi. What worried me was whether he would allow me to continue my Legion work. I told myself I would prefer to stay in Elobi and keep being a Legionary rather than go to a mansion where I couldn't fellowship, as I found joy in the group. That evening, I shared my intentions with my cousin and family. Some were very excited, while others wondered whether he was an occultist.

But because I had known him long before, I assured them it was God's intervention. They cautioned me that in Yaoundé, many blood circles and enslavement exist where people use others for money rituals. I told myself that God could not abandon me in such a situation, for Okafor and his manager had tried in vain. I reminded myself of the blessings the notables of my dynasty had given me and the ones I received from my family before I left for Yaoundé. I finally moved into a two-room apartment in the Cite-Vert neighbourhood one Sunday, carrying just a few things because the flood had destroyed almost everything.

It was a self-contained studio, sophisticatedly furnished with a beautiful set of red leather chairs in the parlour, an embroidered carpet at the centre, a box at one side of the room that contained a TV and a DVD player, and a small dining table at the other side, decorated with a gorgeous vase of enticing artificial flowers that seemed to appeal to everyone who saw them and had a pleasant fragrance. Entering there felt like entering heaven, with the blinds creating a special effect as they swayed gently with the breeze. As I stood there daydreaming, he immediately took me to the bedroom, and as I walked through this state-of-the-art décor, I wondered whether such heaven could exist on earth, too!

I thought it would be all about feelings until I saw the snow-white bed sheet spread on the bed I was to sleep on. I thought, *"Make who sleep for where? Humm, my God, I go just sleep me for floor oooh, make that bed sheet no change colour because of me."* It was only when he laughed at me and said, "No worry, this is your home," that I realized I had said it aloud for him to hear. He added that he would get me some new clothes the following day. What caught my attention was the empty crucifix hung above the bed. I was about to ask for an explanation when I remembered that for Presbyterians, the crucifix is bare because Christ had been taken down from the cross, so He does not need to be there. It is their doctrine. It did not surprise me because I had once been one of them and had gone through such teachings as well. I also noticed the Bible and some Christian literature on the little cupboard beside the bed, which comforted me.

That evening, we ate what was at home, studied the Bible, and then prayed before sleeping. Psalms 4 touched me and was so consoling because it led us to a quiet night. It was clear that I was on the right track and that God had intervened in my life because not all who say,

"Lord, Lord," will enter the kingdom of God, but only those who do the will of God (Matthew 7:21-23). My father once advised me that when you separate from a friend for more than three months, verify well to ensure the person is still who he was because human beings change like chameleons. At night, my mind raced in all directions, wondering how marvellous the power of God is to have led me to that juncture. Once it was daytime, we went shopping for new clothes. When we finished, he asked me to return home and rest, adding to the three-day rest he had given me to gather some energy to join him after these days in supplying goods to his customers. I spent these days praying and asking God to vindicate me from all my challenges forever and, above all, to touch his heart to allow me to continue my church and legionary duties because I knew God had brought me there.

After three days, he revealed the new program we had to follow together to succeed. Our discussions were amicable because I testified that I could not compromise my faith, and he agreed with me, saying it is only God who has led him through many challenges, so he would not tamper with anything that concerns Him because He is the owner of everything we have. I was so happy and assured, and I thanked him heartily. He then asked me to draw up a program on how I would work since I had to take care of the Cadets of Mary and carry out my legionary duties, which I did, and he validated until further notice, as things could change with time. Betterman had many customers in Yaoundé to whom he supplied seasonal goods depending on their demand. He was like a jack of all trades who had almost everything a customer needed.

He mostly got his goods from Onitsha, Nigeria. He took time to show me all his customers and their locations during our deliveries so that I would become familiar with them, know their sales points, and collect debts when he was not around and deposit them in the Ntarikon Credit Union. As we worked and prayed together, the business prospered, and I could carry out my Christian duties without any problems. On Sundays, he would go for church service at the Presbyterian Church in Bastos, where Rev. Pastor Bame was the parish pastor, and at 4 p.m., he would go again for revival service. I attended Sunday Mass at Elig-Efa, where Rev. Fr. Betene was the Parish Priest.

In 1997, we decided to open a shop in Melen since the business was growing. We opened an iron container shop in Njo Melen and later transferred to a bigger house in Ntongolo. We stocked the shop with kitchen utensils and other assorted household goods. This shop was named Betterman's Enterprise. My duties then doubled to that of a manager and night watch. I had to sleep at the shop to prevent thieves from breaking in. Sometimes, I could have a sound sleep, but most of the time, I slept on guard due to the noise and footsteps of thieves struggling to break into our shop. As soon as they realized that someone was inside, they would take to their heels. Melen and Mini-firm were notorious areas for bandits. Most of them respected and protected us due to Betterman's generosity, and they assured us not to be afraid. The more the business grew, the more we needed additional help, so Betterman employed a man and a woman to join me at the shop, and he also took in some family members he sponsored in school, especially since he had plans to get married. We always started and ended our day with prayers. There was no day we would open without first praying, let alone lock up without handing everything to God.

Just as we confided everything we had to deal with in the shop to God, so, too, did we take his project of marriage to the Lord in prayer, asking Him to find the right partner? In early 1998, God answered our prayers and blessed him with a beautiful, responsible, and motherly woman named Constance. She became a mother to us and has cared for us like a mother to this day, remaining a wonderful presence in our lives because she is a kind woman. Constance also contributed to the growth of our business. As a university graduate, she works at the taxation office, which helped us tremendously in our endeavours. Constance is a prayerful woman and excels in her career, as evidenced by numerous promotions. God has uplifted her at every point to where she is today. I concluded that with God through prayer, we could have everything without soiling our hands (Luke 1:37).

Spiritually, our Christian group continued to spread the Legion and Cadets of Mary in the Anglophone communities of Yaoundé, Mbalmayo, and Ebolowa. We also organized small Christian communities in various neighbourhoods in Yaoundé. My interest in the things of God outweighed anything else in this world. Even the business I was managing and the people I encountered wondered whether I was a priest, pastor, or businessman. They stated that no man could juggle business and fully work for God, advising me to choose a path. They were partly right. It was ultimately for God to decide, so I thought, but at that time, it was what it was.

In late 1998, when I was nearing the end of my time with Betterman, the Yaoundé Urban Council destroyed shops on Melen Street after midnight. I heard knocks at our door: "Betterman, Betterman, come out!" I woke up, but with the noise coming from the crowd, I knew something serious was happening. As I walked out, many people were crying as they had already destroyed three shops before ours. According to them, they had asked us to evacuate the premises because they wanted to expand the road, but since we were proving stubborn, it warranted their nocturnal destruction.

That night, they had called Betterman, and he was already there. It was also that same night that I witnessed the greatest miracle from God because I cried out that we had dedicated the shop and our lives to Him. How could He allow this to happen just when I was about to gain my independence? Before we had time to remove some goods, the caterpillar had already approached our shop. As it advanced, the engine stopped working. They struggled to get it working again, but as the head lifted, it went high above the caterpillar and then got blocked. When they tried to bring it down, it fell onto the road. We didn't understand what was happening as we stood there crying, but the crowd started shouting, "Fru Ndi, Fru Ndi," repeatedly. The atmosphere became lively; some forgot the sorrow of their lost shops in amazement at what had happened. We heard comments like, *"C'est sont les Bamenda, nor. Tu ne le connais pas. Ils sont fort avec la magie."*

We stood in that crowd, crying and confused. For over ten to fifteen minutes, nothing happened, and their chef de mission asked them to continue with the other shops. We noticed one of them writing something on our container. As soon as they passed our shop, the caterpillar started working again, and they became more brutal in their efforts. The shops they destroyed after ours suffered more losses than the rest. In the end, we just stood there staring. The place looked like a wilderness, with only our shop standing at the centre. As we crossed, we read what they had written on our container: "They said to remove it in 30 minutes." I was sure they were afraid, as some commented that they had never seen such a mystery. That was further proof that God supports those who trust in Him. No matter what people said, we were certain that it was the effect of our prayers that saved us from experiencing tremendous loss that night.

They touched nothing, not even a pin, in our shop. We opened it and removed the goods that night. The bandits in the quarter all came out to assist and ensure security as we transferred the goods to Betterman's aunt's house in Mini-Firm. Instead of 30 minutes, the container remained there for three more days until we removed it ourselves. This demonstrated that wherever we were, the presence of God prevailed, making people believe in Him. I was happy staying at home for a month, where I relaxed and felt free, as it was not as cramped in the container while we searched for a new shop.

God blessed us, and we found a more spacious shop at *Marché Melen*, this time in a big building. Most Bamileke business people approached Betterman to find out what magic he used to secure the shop. With the assistance of the Ntarikon Credit Union, we stocked the shop to capacity, and in the end, we had a bigger and more beautiful shop on that street. This time, we decided I would no longer sleep in the shop to guard it; we hired a night watchman. That was an *"au revoir"* to the pains of leaving Tongolo-Etoudi every night to go to Melen for *"gardienage."*

While I took care of the new shop, Betterman began to discuss settling me down, which brought me nightmares as I did not know the outcome. I worried about how much he would give me, how I would start my own business, and what I would do. Betterman told me to settle down and be independent. He added that our being together had been a blessing. My mind returned to my life in Bamenda and what I went through with the small shop I opened. I prayed not to face the same situation again and that things would always be good. Betterman proposed our former shop. The landlady suggested she could build shops instead of using containers in that area if I had the money.

That was the best option, and in January 1999, I received FCFA 1.5 million in the presence of my friends, Betterman's friends, and a few other important people to start a business. He appreciated our time together and advised me to be careful because my style of serving God might not allow me to progress in my business journey. He added that when he looked at me, he saw a priest, not a businessman. He also appreciated my financial transparency, encouraging me to continue like that, for God would show me the way. He promised to assist me in building a small shop and asked me to stay with him until I settled down. We finished constructing the shop and paid rent for the space for six months.

I prepared to fix and stock the place to start a business. This time, I asked the legionaries to pray for me more than ever. I was happy I had mastered the town and knew many businesspeople. I had also made a name in the church. Betterman was right; I needed to work full-time to make the business grow, but my desire to go out for evangelical work was strong. It was a battle. I realized it was easy to be a manager and complicated to be a master because, as the master, you plan everything, from paying taxes to taking care of yourself and handling other responsibilities that come with that role.

At this point, I realized that I had not mastered business tactics but had focused more on spiritual matters, as the Cadets of Mary had grown to over 700 members. I was thankful to have served another master who appreciated and recognized me as someone capable of doing great things, particularly in serving God. I did not know where to start, as I was merely a primary school leaver. I found joy working as a Christian but never became a priest. However, there was a force within me that made me want to talk to people about God. Before starting my business, I decided to visit my people in Bamenda and the village to inform them of what I had become. It was a beautiful experience.

Chapter XIII - My Turning Point

Being with Betterman was a blessing because I could now tend to my shop, knowing God was with me. The spiritual director of the Legion of Mary at the time, Rev. Fr. Patrick Adeso, a lecturer at the *Université Catholique de l'Afrique Centrale (UCAC)* in Nkolbisson, Yaoundé, came to bless the shop on its opening day, accompanied by some legionaries, Betterman, and other Christians. I named it "The Consecrated." It was a glorious moment for me. I praised God for His glorious deeds, as reflected in Psalms 145. To honour my time with Betterman and to better manage the business, I rented a studio that was still under construction in the Melen neighbourhood. This also helped reduce transportation costs and allowed me to keep a close watch over the shop. I started timidly with kitchen utensils and other accessories. I attended daily Mass at Njoh Melen Parish to keep my faith alive and remain focused on my purpose, so I would not be easily distracted by the business from the things of God.

In May 1999, responsibilities began to set in. They ranged from paying rent and taxes to caring for needy family members. The pressure of these responsibilities was heavy, as it never seemed to stop. It felt like a planned act that did not want to let me rest. Problems came in succession; once I finished solving one, another flashed before me. Sometimes they arrived in pairs—all equally important—so I had to find ways to address them. Solving problems became second nature to me. I am passionate about helping those in need, and I cannot help but feel compassion each time they share their struggles with me. My prayer has always been for Him to bless me so that I can take care of humanity, especially those in dire need.

The little shop became a miracle point where commercial activities were not just the order of the day; it was also a place where people came for counselling and prayers. I had an inner zeal for anyone who walked into my shop to know God. As a result, I preached the Word to everyone who entered. Parents, couples, children, families, and people from all walks of life came for counselling, whether for themselves, their children, or their friends. I closed the shop every Saturday at 3 p.m. to work with the Cadets of Mary, as I did each time I had legion work. Sundays were among my busiest days. After Mass, we engaged in various spiritual activities, from visiting other parishes all over Yaoundé, Mbalmayo, and Ebolowa to monitoring the functioning of the Cadet and Legionary groups. The workload was so heavy that sometimes I returned home by midnight.

In the Legion of Mary, we are sent out like the apostles—in pairs—to visit families, hospitals, the sick, and the needy, and to encourage lukewarm members in the life of the sacraments (Matt 10:1-12). We experienced many miracles during these visits. The Blessed Virgin Mary inspired me to write a book titled "The Consecrated to Mary," which remains incomplete to this day. In it, I discuss how the Army of Mary is fighting spiritual battles in this world, with Mary as their commander. As a disciple of the Blessed Virgin Mary, I discovered that she, too, has many enemies in the world, even within the Catholic Church, and especially in new religious movements of which I had once been a member. I realized that God made her the crusher of the head of the serpent (Gen 3:15), how she fought against the dragon (Rev 12:1-6), and how her children and believers in Christ continue to battle (Rev 12:17).

I vowed to make her known to the world as the most loved, most honoured, and most privileged mother of our Savior, Queen of Heaven, and Queen of the Apostles. In the Cameroon Hymnal, she has more than forty titles, which no human being has ever possessed. It is an honour from heaven and gives me great consolation in working for God. It made me think maybe Betterman was right when he said, "You better become a reverend father, for there will be no real business success for anyone who works like me." It felt like a dream, especially considering that I only had the First School Certificate. I laughed at the thought, particularly when I considered the number of years seminarians study to become priests.

Life in UCAC

These previous thoughts flooded my mind with many questions: "Did I miss my way? Why didn't I further my education?" I blamed my father, who wanted me to be a herdsman instead of sending me to school, and later sent me to a Nigerian businessman who robbed me of precious time. No matter how much I pretended not to have a burning desire for God, it grew stronger. I prayed that God would show me the way. When I took stock at the end of that year, I discovered I barely made a profit; I was almost at a deficit. But each time, I told myself that the next time would be better and that I should concentrate on business, but I was fooling myself. I struggled throughout the year until the worst happened on the night of May 5, 2000. Armed robbers had dug a hole into the shop from the wall behind and took away virtually everything. I did not know until after morning Mass when I came out and saw people crying in front of the shop, pointing to the back.

When I arrived at the scene, I was confused about whether to cry, scream, run, or hide. I just felt tears running down my cheeks, and I quickly left the place for my studio. From that day until the end of the week, many people visited to console me. They were legionaries, Christians, and friends. It was a bitter pill to swallow because, to me, it did not feel real. I was still waiting to wake up from what I described as a nightmare. Finally, I had to accept that it was not a dream and that I had to face reality. I no longer had a space where I could receive people for prayers or counselling, nor did I have money for rent, my upkeep, or even for those I had promised to help. I concluded that life is, indeed, a mystery that we search for and will keep searching for answers until we return to our Savior.

I realized that we stop living once we stop asking questions about life. I remembered Job, who endured the worst and spent time asking questions until he found answers in God, who ultimately blessed him (Job 1 & 39). Reflecting on this, I wondered if my situation would be similar. I didn't know the answers, but deep within me, I concluded that He held the answers to all the questions swirling in my mind. I was still confused, and Betterman immediately rebuilt the place while waiting to find a way to restock the shop. I didn't know how it would happen, but Betterman contacted some businessmen who imported second-hand goods from Germany. He gave me some items on credit to stock the shop, with the understanding that I would pay him back as I sold them. Unfortunately, it did not work out, as the importers already had buyers ready to pay cash.

I tried to mend my wounds as much as I could, but as time passed, I found myself in June that year with dysfunctional second-hand goods that were impossible to sell unless first repaired. That is how I started spending money I didn't even have, fixing items to make them marketable. I was shocked to find even Christians advising me to consult witch doctors, concluding that it could be the result of a curse upon me, especially since I came from the palace. I almost fell into the temptation of believing they were right and that I needed special prayers.

From then on, I began experiencing hostility from my landladies (both for the shop and studio). They started disturbing me and never gave me peace, even though I still had two months left before the rent was due. The best people could tell me was that this was the usual behaviour of Ewondo Eton landlords. Some even went as far as removing the door when they were hungry and poor. They advised me that as a tenant, I had to appease them by regularly giving them gifts, or I would wake up one day to find another person renting my shop and house. They added that, no matter how much money they had, Eton and Ewondo landlords complained of poverty because their extravagant lifestyles drained them dry before the month's end. I saw why our economy cannot grow due to such a wasteful way of living in this country.

To survive, I also tried offering home classes for pupils, but most of the time, the parents never paid. It was thanks to the help I received from some legionaries and Christians that I managed to make ends meet. As time dragged on, I struggled in vain until the day I met the legion's spiritual director, Rev. Fr. Adeso. After listening to my story, he told me clearly that the Lord was calling me to His vineyard and that I should further my education. He gave me FCFA twenty thousand to enroll in a school, eighteen to nineteen years after I had completed primary school. What preoccupied my mind at the time was where I would begin. I spent sleepless nights worrying and praying, asking God to show me the way forward. Though I was in confusion and pain, my studio became a consultation ground for Christians as they brought their problems to counselling.

My younger brothers, some of whom were almost university graduates—Kum George, Meh Christian, and Kum Rene—assured me that it was never too late to return to school, quoting examples of people who returned to school at 80 and completed their education. My main concern was what would become of the shop and whether I would be able to repay my loans, especially to those who had given me goods. I finally received advice from some businessmen, with Betterman being one of them, as the mental burden was already too much for me.

They all confirmed that I could not survive in business by dedicating all my time to God. Betterman reiterated that he had mentioned this before and advised me to follow the path the Lord had set for me, as prescribed by the priest. I realized that deep within me, there was nothing that could work in my life except serving in the Lord's vineyard. That was what brought me joy, and I concluded that the most essential thing in life is to be happy, whether rich or poor, old or young, educated or uneducated. I also concluded that most people do not know the secret to happiness because they chase after the things of this world. All of this gave me the courage to forge ahead with my inner calling.

Having gathered the necessary energy, along with the conviction of following the path laid out for me by the Lord, I started searching for a school. In December 2000, I registered as an external candidate for the Ordinary Level (O/L) at Government Bilingual High School (GBHS) Essos. It was a dramatic experience for many who thought I was there to register my child. They were shocked when they found out I was doing so for myself. Even though my brothers trained me and carefully explained the procedure, I still got confused when implementing it. It was thanks to some students who recognized me as a member of St. Joseph Parish Mvog-Ada that I was able to complete the registration formalities.

A fellow legionary, Sis Emma, who taught at GBHS Essos, helped me fill out the registration form. She also advised me to register in an evening school to prepare for the exams, as she was shocked and scandalized to discover I was merely a primary school leaver. To her, I needed to register in a school to gain the necessary skills and knowledge, even though there were only six months left. It was only after I completed my registration that my mind began to function normally. I questioned how I could register myself without first returning to school. I wondered which rational person would begin a process at the end of the game without considering the introduction. I had no clue about the content of all the subjects, making it imperative to be admitted to a school before it was too late.

I finally enrolled in Promoter Evening School at Carrefour EMIA Yaoundé. It was a significant challenge for me. I did not know what kind of miracle would enable my success. I hurriedly borrowed the books from my classmates to catch up while my brothers tutored me at home. They helped me understand my notes and revise past GCE questions, which I had bought. I prayed more than ever before to the Holy Spirit and the Blessed Virgin Mary to give me strength in this new venture. I was determined to make the Lord known if I succeeded.

To meet my financial needs, I bought a *chinchin* machine, which allowed me to produce chinchin for sale in shops and sometimes for events. It was a real battle, but I knew that with God, it would work. The words of Vincent Norman Peale in his book The Power of Positive Thinking, where he quotes Philippians 4:13—"I can do all things through Christ"—resonated with me. He also said, "The bigger your problem, the bigger your faith and prayer because someone trained in prayer can overcome all challenges." I identified with this because, throughout my life, prayer has seen me through, bringing me to where I am today.

I studied hard day and night. The *chinchin* business was indeed a great help, but it did not change the fact that I still had huge debts pending, along with the reality that most of my income was tied up with some of my customers who owed me for the *chinchin* I had supplied. This indicated that I was not cut out for business, but then, how would I survive?

In June, on the day of the English Literature session, my landlady arrived early that morning with three gendarmes to throw out my belongings, even though I still had a month left to stay. It was a scandal in the entire neighbourhood, as all my neighbours came out to watch the scene. I was still at home at 7 a.m. sorting things out, with some items already thrown outside.

If not for the intervention of Mr. Fouda Lucas, the landlady's son, and his wife, Agnes, who lived in the same building, I do not know what would have become of me. The temptations were overwhelming. He quarrelled with his mother before I could take my exams, insisting that they would help pack my things back into their apartment. That day, I arrived at the examination centre 45 minutes late and confused. I could not find my exam hall. Sis Emma saw me as I almost walked into the hall where she was invigilating. She helped me locate my hall and intervened with the invigilator to allow me entry. As I walked in, I felt all eyes on me. The students looked at me inquisitively while the invigilator told me that were it not for Sis Emma, he would have suspended me. He then showed me to a seat.

Thank God I finished writing that subject even before the end of the session, but I could not escape the questions from the other students, who flooded me with inquiries about why I was so late. I could not give them an answer; all I wanted was to go home and sort my things out. They gave me a small room in the Fouda family house, where I could stay until further notice. I became the son of that house while waiting for the result of the GCE. Shortly after that, toward the end of July, the mother gave birth to a son they named Gabriel. I was privileged to be chosen as the Godfather.

Despite the challenges I faced, people did not stop coming over for spiritual counselling until the Fouda home resembled a spiritual centre where everyone could seek guidance. I could receive about twenty people a day, and everyone was surprised that an Ewondo man would allow people to walk in and out of his house so freely. But deep down, I believed it was the work of God. Thank God some of these Christians were people of goodwill, as they provided us with financial and material assistance, which helped me survive. I dedicated much time to my missionary work with the Legion of Mary, visiting small Christian communities and the Cadets of Mary.

Sadly, some people who came to me for counselling wondered why I was received by the Foudas, especially since, as the saying goes, I was nobody to them—not their relative, not even a friend or someone from their village. They went so far as to urge the Foudas to kick me out. But the Foudas rebuked them for being unkind to an innocent soul. At the beginning of August, I grew anxious while waiting for the GCE results. I wondered what the outcome would be. And it happened! Jesus, the Wonder Worker, blessed me—I passed four subjects! It was a cause for celebration. Everyone who knew me celebrated as if I had received 11 A's, assuring me that I was on the right path.

The following month, parishioners of St. Joseph Anglophone Parish Mvog-Ada Yaoundé organized a Thanksgiving Mass in my honour, and about 300 people came to celebrate with me. The joy was overwhelming. Some commented, "Our priest in the making." This success felt like the final word from God, confirming that I had chosen the right path and needed to continue to the end. That day, many people testified about my journey, expressing heartfelt gratitude. I appreciated all those who contributed, in one way or another, to my success, reminding them that the real battle with God was still ahead and that we would conquer. I understood that doing good rather than harm could overcome any battle, so I was determined to do good and avoid harm to achieve my destiny (Psalm 1: 1-6).

Chapter XIV - My Final Yes To God's Call

My success in the GCE Ordinary Level changed the course of my life. I felt happy and assured by God that the best thing to do was to serve Him. I asked myself: if people could celebrate my success in that manner, how would they celebrate if I made it to the Advanced Level or entered the Seminary? This thought motivated me to hurry to the next step.

In early September 2001, I enrolled in Matamfen Evening High School at Rond Point Nlongkak in Yaoundé, as Madam Fouda was a teacher who would resume teaching that September. We agreed that I would babysit Cabriel while she was in school during the day, and then I would attend school in the evenings after she returned. Babysitting, making *chinchin*, and reading at the same time was not easy.

I realized that with humility, one can provide services that many would consider impossible, as going from being a businessman to becoming a babysitter and *chinchin* seller would come as a shock to many proud individuals. It brought back memories of when my father held me back to look after one of my sisters when I was supposed to start primary school, slowing me down for a whole year. That was in the past; I now had to concentrate on the task ahead.

It was a privilege to care for an innocent child and witness how I nurtured him into manhood. It was a real school of life, as I learned the language of innocent babies. I knew when the baby had pooped, was hungry, felt sleepy, or was unwell. I also learned what to give him to cleanse his stomach of dirt or worms and that I shouldn't carry him for too long, for he might become too accustomed to being held and consequently shy away from the bed.

This experience made me a defender of innocent babies and young children, especially when I witnessed the brutality and indifference some adults showed toward them. I recalled how Pharaoh slaughtered all the Israelite male children in Egypt out of jealousy and fear, and how some pagans offered their little ones to their gods as sacrifices. I also remembered how Herod, in Matthew 2, killed all male children aged two years and under out of fear of being dethroned by the newborn king. I cannot forget the dragon in Revelation 12:1-6, where the devil waited patiently to devour Baby Jesus when he was about to be born.

It is also painful to know that some parents today, even among married couples, still abort their babies for reasons such as not being prepared, lacking financial resources, or being unmarried, among many other absurd justifications.

This explains why there are many curses in the world due to the massacre of innocent souls (Deut. 27:24-26). Throughout that year, it was not easy, yet I ventured to register for the GCE A/L. This time, I failed the exam but passed one paper and received a compensatory grade in another. That was in 2002. Despite the failure, I still decided to offer a Thanksgiving Mass to God, as it was not the only thing I had achieved that year. I learned many things and discovered others. At the end of the Mass, when Rev. Lucien Betene announced the Mass intention, the congregation was sad and amazed at how I could thank God for a failure.

Meanwhile, I was happy that I passed one paper and received a compensatory grade. It was an achievement for me, as it was not the only thing I gained that year. I realized that people only thank God for the good things that happen in their lives. When circumstances change and they face the trials and hardships that life brings, they do not realize that these are also moments to thank the Lord. I experienced many positive outcomes each time I thanked God during trying moments. It is always good to try.

That year, my family decided to hire a babysitter so I could enrol in a day school. In September 2002, I registered as a day student at English High School in Quartier Obili, Yaoundé, where I had to wear a uniform and sit in class to learn. It was a tough decision, but I needed to pray for more humility to endure that and achieve higher goals. In this life, when you know what you are looking for, there should be no complexity. Though it was a tough decision, it was the best one.

In college from 2001 to 2003

My responsibilities at the time crowded me with many activities, making it hard to prepare for examinations.

Becoming a day student allowed me to grapple with my studies, and legion activities, and attend to those who came to me for advice on spiritual matters. At first, things seemed to be moving smoothly, but over time, it became more challenging to manage. As an Arts student, I had to dedicate most of my time to reading, but whenever I picked up my notes, someone would come in with a problem. Additionally, I had accumulated legion work and many other activities, making it harder to handle the situation. Being a day student was a new reality for me, something I had never experienced for more than 20 years. Sitting in class with students who were more like my children and some teachers who were my juniors was challenging. Most teachers addressed me as Mr. Christopher instead of using my first name.

Sometimes, I received preferential treatment, and they hardly punished me for anything. Even when I arrived late, I was allowed in while other latecomers had to stand at the gate. I was never insulted or beaten for failing a subject. This sometimes disturbed me, and my conscience would torment me, especially when I was at fault or when I suspected teachers were referring to me indirectly. Some even recommended textbooks that could help me and told me to feel free to consult them if I didn't understand anything in their subjects.

The task became increasingly tedious for me, particularly as I had to manage many extracurricular activities, which ultimately pushed me to abandon my chinchin business in an attempt to keep up. Thank God for the kind souls who helped me meet my needs during this period. Nevertheless, the weight of my responsibilities significantly affected my studies, as was evident when I failed the mock exams. The school authority had to summon the parents and guardians of all those who did not perform well in the mock exams to avoid a low percentage in the GCE.

When the Foudas received this invitation, they felt worried and embarrassed. They agreed that the mother of the house would represent the family. When it was my turn to answer what had hindered me from succeeding in my exams, Mama Agnes told them that I spent more time doing God's work and counselling than studying. Even though she was my mom by responsibility, she was younger than me, and I owed my life to them for being such wonderful parents. The school administration advised me to dedicate more time to my studies since the A/L is not as simple as O/L; the A/L is more analytical than narrative. For my benefit and that of the school, they mandated the Foudas to implement some restrictions until after the GCE, after which I could do as I pleased. They enforced these restrictions effectively, instructing people to let me be until I completed the exams.

Another option was to study with a group of students in a quiet and calm place, like the school, after closing hours instead of studying at home. These restrictions and commitments to studying facilitated my progress. I recognized what being a real student meant after these limitations. I understood that trying to juggle many things at once would never be as effective or rewarding as concentrating on a few tasks at a time, doing them well, and achieving better results. I realized that most people fail because they attempt to handle more than they can manage. They start a project and, shortly after, jump to another without proper planning. Some Christians engage in five or more groups and are nowhere to be found. Even in families, parents are often absent because they are too busy chasing money. Such people are called "Jacks of all trades and masters of none."

As June approached, the intensity of my studies increased, and thoughts about the outcome worried me. Most Christians who knew me were supportive of my decision to move to the seminary, and my dreams of becoming a priest grew stronger. Rev. Fr. Adeso was ready to recommend me as soon as I finished writing the GCE. The three-week session began in June. When we finished, I met Fr. Adeso and expressed my wish to become a priest in the Douala Archdiocese, as that was where I felt the Lord was leading me. However, he advised me to apply to Bertoua, where they would accept me despite my age. After a few days, I received a recommendation letter from him addressed to Mgr. Roger Pirenne, the Bishop of the Archdiocese of Bertoua. Although this was not my preference, as I believed God was calling me to the Douala Archdiocese, I had no choice but to accept.

Meanwhile, Mr. Fouda and some Christians insisted on pursuing my acceptance into the Archdiocese of Yaoundé instead of my preferred choice, arguing that our parish priest at the time, Fr. Betene, could facilitate the procedure. However, I remained firm in my choice of Douala and nowhere else. Only Mama Fouda understood me and asked them to let me be, as they were not the ones to answer my call. Mama Agnes urged that I be allowed to go where the Spirit was leading me.

When I arrived at the Bishop's House in Bertoua, I was told that the letter was meant for the Bishop of Gabon instead of Bertoua. I realized that it was God at work. I took the letter to Rev. Adeso, who was shocked to discover it was not for the Archbishop of Bertoua but for the Bishop of Gabon, wondering how he could have made such a grave mistake. For me, it was not a mistake but rather God intervening on my behalf. Before we knew it, it was already August, making it too late for me to apply for admission to any diocese because Rev. Fr. Adeso was a busy man. He was an international professor, travelling regularly, which made it difficult to rectify the mistake in time for me to submit my application.

Finally, the long-awaited results came out, and God blessed me with three A/L papers and a compensatory. I was overwhelmed and worshipped the Lord even more. Crowds gathered to congratulate me, and I offered a Thanksgiving Mass. We all celebrated the joy, especially the Foudas, who were extremely happy. That was another step toward fulfilling the Will of God in my life. I thanked them all for their support and prayers and praised the Lord. This time, the joy I felt was different; looking back, I realized that I had put in a lot of hard work and had invested much more energy than I had during the O/L. It taught me that succeeding after toiling and investing in something generates a different kind of inner joy and satisfaction. Reaping the fruits of genuine and sincere labour is a blessing. I did not hesitate to apply immediately to the Catholic University of Central Africa (UCAC) in Nkolbisson, where Rev. Fr. Adeso taught scriptures. I had no idea where the fees would come from. This decision led to mockery, as people questioned whether I was in my right senses to apply to such an expensive university when I had no funds, especially when there were state universities with tuition of just FCFA 50,000.

It did not move me because I had faith in the one who held my destiny. The estimated budget for the school amounted to FCFA 1.5 million annually. The Lord inspired me to write requests to three families (Mr. & Mrs. Okeke, Mr. & Mrs. Galega, and Mr. & Mrs. Ndum Augustine) for sponsorship. It was a miracle that they all agreed to help with so much joy. When the school administration asked me to deposit 60 per cent of the tuition before October 2003, the families immediately rallied and raised the money. Part of what they gave me was used for textbooks. I was in the Faculty of Philosophy, and it was ironic to be studying in French when all I knew was what I had learned on the streets during my business period. However, there seemed to be a spirit within me that always assured me that nothing is impossible with God (Luke 1:37), and I told myself I would succeed come rain or shine.

I began preparing for the new academic year with a lot of zeal. Looking back at my life, I felt that only the Trinity could perform such wonders as He did in Egypt through Moses. I realized that faith in Jesus Christ is freedom, not living according to the opinions of others that differ from the will of the one who created them. My focus on listening to my Master, Jesus Christ, rather than listening to men was a determining factor. I was confident that studying at a Catholic university would pave better ways for me to enter the priesthood. When schools resumed in early October, I was still commuting from Melen to Nkolbisson.

The first months were tedious because of the distance. I spent a lot on transportation, going through many stops before reaching my destination. Additionally, the people who came for consultations could not allow me to study; they flooded the house, making it difficult for me to touch my books. This made me realize that I needed an urgent solution to engage in my studies. I presented this difficulty to my sponsors, who immediately rallied to get a room for me near the school campus. I was amazed by their quick intervention and the speed with which they secured a room at that time of the academic year when almost all hostels were full. They paid the rent for one year. I did not need another miracle, for I was already experiencing them every second. This indicated that my path and destiny were open, and I was the only one who could spoil it by becoming distracted.

When I finally settled into my room, I could feel that I was now a university student and would have to face the challenges that came with it. In a class of 35 students, I was the only lay Christian; the rest were religious and seminarians. The task was very challenging. Studying in French, translating into English, photocopying notes, and doing research was a nightmare. No matter how tough it got, I knew I could make it through because I had virtually everything I needed to concentrate on my studies. It was amazing. Studying with seminarians and religious was edifying; they helped me find my way, and everyone wanted to assist me. Despite the difficulties, I made it through my exams without much trouble, and my results were good. Thanks to the environment and the support of those around me, I had a better understanding of what was taught, which helped me during my exams as I answered questions in English, despite receiving lectures in French.

The only course that tortured me in Philosophy was Logic, which kept requiring me to re-sit the exam. After the first year, I considered myself a student at that prestigious university. Nevertheless, I continued seeking admission to a seminary in the Douala Archdiocese. Being a student in the Faculty of Philosophy was advantageous because they teach philosophy in the seminary. When I could not validate Cosmology and Logic in the second year, I switched to the Faculty of Theology so as not to lose that year, since one could not move forward without validating all the courses. I was preparing to start a new academic year in Theology when Rev. Fr. Adeso was discovered dead in his apartment after three days. His death was and still is shrouded in mystery. It was a big shock and a blow to me. I was unable to do anything as I was in deep mourning. Friends and classmates consoled me, but what gave me the strength to move forward was when I reminded myself that if God permitted it, He must have a better plan, for God knows best.

While in Theology, I studied hard to re-sit the last two courses that blocked me from achieving my Pontifical Certificate. For those who do not understand, the university has a peculiar way of functioning. Studying for two years is equivalent to three years of studies in the seminary, so entering the third year is considered a different cycle. In basic terms, we receive a degree after two years, and entering the third year is like entering the master's cycle.

Returning to my situation, I re-sat for the two courses while continuing my studies, this time in Theology. Thankfully, I succeeded in Cosmology. It seemed that Logic had a grudge against me, as it still held me back. It was only after re-sitting it for the second time that I validated it, and behold, I had finally completed all the requirements to obtain a Pontifical Certificate. The Logic professor, David Eleba, congratulated me for my patience and determination. Validating the course felt like removing a hook from my throat.

While in Theology, several people (Mr. & Mrs. Galega and my Godmother, Fanso Ansela) met with His Eminence Christian Cardinal Tumi, who was Chancellor of the Catholic University at that time, to present my case for admission into his archdiocese. After listening to them with interest, he said I would need a recommendation letter from my Godmother since she is a catechist. Given that universities do not form priests—only seminaries do—I asked the Vicar General of the Yaoundé Archdiocese and parish priest of St. Joseph Anglophone Parish at the time, Mgr. Befe Ateba, for a recommendation, which he provided without hesitation.

The Cardinal asked for my Theology results after I completed the first year so he could verify if the courses taught matched those of the seminary. He also requested recommendation letters and other required documents for admission to the seminary. I met with him after Theology I, and he asked me to leave my documents with the secretary and wait for a call to find out if I had been accepted. Meeting the Cardinal face to face was a privilege for me because he was my life model. He was a man of his word and principles who spoke the truth without hesitation. Most of the people I encountered who spoke about him had benefited from his greatness, and I was no exception.

I decided to emulate some of his virtues to defend the voiceless and vulnerable in the world. Waiting for the call that would make my dream come true was not easy; the wait felt too long, almost like a century. Nightmares dominated my sleep, and I wondered if I would be accepted. What would it look like? Who would I meet there? Had I made the best choice? It was true when my classmates and seminarians told me it would be a miracle if they accepted me because of my age. I spent a lot of time in my room and at the university chapel in prayer. I requested prayers from priests and seminarians at the Catholic University, especially the Legionaries and Cadets of Mary, and particularly from my sponsors.

To my greatest amazement, my Godmother searched for me, saying that I had an urgent letter from Cardinal Tumi. When I heard this, I almost lost my composure. My heart was racing as I wondered what the letter would be about. Immediately, I went to see her in Messa, where she was living. The letter was about my admission to Paul VI Major Seminary Douala. Schools would begin on October 5, 2006, and I had been admitted to the second-year Theology class. The letter made my Godmother and I shed tears of joy, and those present celebrated in happiness. Though it was a dream come true, I had no clue what awaited me. Those who knew me celebrated when they heard the news; for them, that was where I belonged. The news spread like wildfire, and some people who called to congratulate me left me wondering how they had heard. I had to get my things ready because October 5 was approaching. At the same time, I planned a send-off Mass with the help of my sponsors. Some kind souls assisted me with material and financial gifts. It was a highly attended Mass, and most people shed joyful tears and praised God for His marvels, whose love and mercy are abundant for the poor and needy. My journey was well prepared, as I received many gifts in cash and kind. On October 5, as early as 4 a.m., I left for Douala to start my seminary studies.

Glossary: Pidgin English And French Words and Phrases

- *Njangi*: Popular meaning; rotatory savings in pidgin English

- *Twenty hungry*: The most difficult period of the month before salaries

- *Na so my own things di always bi*: That is always my case

- *Over my die bodi, my pikin no fit be nganankoh*: Over my dead body, my son cannot be a shepherd.

- *Yi get plenty pikin ndem, make yi send ndem for go doam*: He has many sons, let him choose one of them to do it.

- *If patron bi dey there when that tin happens, something terrible for happen*: If the boss were here when that happened, it would have been terrible.

- *Where patron yi madam dey*: Where is the boss's wife?

- *Madam no di stay here, she did do business for Nigeria and she fit come here one time in many years*: Madam lives in Nigeria and only comes to visit once in a while.

- *Na because oga want to be going after small Cameroonian girls weh make him leave madam for Nigeria*: It is because the boss wants to flirt with young girls that is why he left his wife in Nigeria.

- *Prise de contacte:*" First time meeting someone.

- *Carabot*: A blank house.

- *Calé calé*: Police and or Gendarme raids.

- *Abeg una leave me ya*: Please, let me be.

- *Wety be legion of Mary sef*: What is the Legion of Mary all about?

- *"Christopher, wety you di do for here:"* Christopher, what are you doing here?

- *"C'est surement son ami qui n'est pas au pays*: It is surely his friend who lives abroad

- *Sa vie va surement changer, hein*: His will definitely change.

- *Na life*: That is life

- *Make who sleep for where?!! Hmm, my God, a go just sleep me for floor oooh, make that bed sheet no change colour because of me*: Who should sleep on such a bed? I will just sleep on the floor so as not to make the bedsheets dirty.

- *C'est sont les Bamenda, nor. Tu ne les connais pas, ils sont fort avec la magie* : Thèse are people frome Bamenda. Don't you know them? They are good in black magic.

- *Chef de mission*: Coordinator.

- *Marché Melen*: Melen Market

About the Author

Reverend Father Christopher Geh Kum is a native of Esu, Wum, in the Menchum Division of the North West Region of Cameroon. Born into a royal family, he is the fifth of twelve children of his polygamous royal father.

He holds a Master's degree in Pastoral Theology from the Loyola Institute in the USA and has written a book titled "A Study Guide for Christian Students and Learners." Bilingual in English and French, Rev. Fr. Christopher Geh Kum is passionate about teaching and guiding people to know God while developing a profound faith in Him. He also enjoys teaching the younger generation to discover their true worth and destiny.

He serves in the Archdiocese of Douala, Cameroon, as the Diocesan Chaplain for the Catholic Women's Association (CWA) and the Saint Jude Apostolate. Additionally, he is the coordinator for the Diocesan Youth and Infants Chaplaincy, as well as the Diocesan Chaplaincy of Vocations and for the Catechists.

Rev. Fr. Christopher Geh Kum also oversees a Vocational Training Centre for Information and Communication Technologies. He is a committed and joyful priest who loves to travel. His greatest endeavour is to help people discover the true worth of life.